Milestones

*Seventeen circular walks exploring mills
and the surrounding landscape in
Oxfordshire and just beyond*

Elaine Steane

Illustrated by
Katie Burt
Dixon Scott
John Steane

2015

Milestones to Millstones: Mill walks in Oxfordshire and beyond
© Elaine Steane
ISBN 978-1-909116-58-0

Published in 2015 by SRA Books

The right of Elaine Steane to be identified as the author
of this work has been asserted by her in accordance
with the Copyright, Designs and Patents Act 1988.

A CIP record of this book is available from the British Library.

All rights reserved. No part of this book may be reproduced, stored
in a retrieval system, or transmitted in any form or by any means,
electronic, mechanical, photocopying, recording or otherwise,
without the prior written permission of the copyright holder.

No responsibility for loss occasioned to any person acting
or refraining from action as a result of any material in this
publication can be accepted by the author or publisher.

Printed in the UK by TJ International, Padstow.

Acknowledgements

Dedicated to John with love

The idea for this project was from Sue Crisp, suggested to me on a snowy morning's walk in 2010 when I was feeling very 'flat' after *The Roman Way* was published. I thank her for that, as this led to so many intriguing and enjoyable walks with friends (members of the Oxfordshire Ramblers, Oxford Fieldpaths Society and the Oxford and District H.F. Rambling Club).

John Eyre helped plan the route of many walks, giving meticulous distances. Brian and Jean Hackett, Robin Harrison, Tony and Leslie Lewis, the late David Muston, Ros Muston, Evelyn Taylor, Christine Tulloch, Virginia Walker and Judy Westgate were among our initial recceing team when we discovered parts of the countryside that we had never walked before.

Then came the task of rechecking the routes. Claire Jeffrey, Eileen Lukes, Neil Monaghan, Colin and Josie Morgan, Anne Partridge, Nick Quartley, Siobhan Stead-Ellis and Jim Stevens rewalked the routes in all weathers and fed back invaluable revisions.

Katie Burt and Julia Cresswell have been my staunch support in researching and preparing the text. My talented husband John has again enlivened the text with his illustrations of the mills. It has meant squatting on a camping stool on windy spots in all seasons. John has also contributed much to the book from his expert knowledge of vernacular architecture. Many of the other illustrations are by the skilful hands of Katie Burt and Dixon Scott.

Janet Redfern and Gilly Graham have carefully proofread the text. A sincere thank you to Marion Stockton for her skilled project management, book production and her ideas for enriching it and to Gerard Little for the maps. There are many other people, not mentioned here by name, including volunteer custodians of the mills, who have helped me in all sorts of ways – thanks to all of you.

Elaine Steane – October 2015

Care for the Countryside

Please respect the Country Code in the following ways:

- Enjoy the route, but keep to the rights of way.
- Close all gates and avoid damage to crops. Please keep away from farm animals.
- To avoid disturbance to wildlife or farm animals, keep your dog under close control at all times, preferably on a lead through fields with animals in. (**N.B.** if you are being harassed by cattle, it may be safer only in this circumstance to let the dog off the lead).
- Please take all your litter home. It looks unsightly and can be dangerous to wildlife and farm animals.
- Take extra care on country roads. Walk on the right side except round blind corners.
- If travelling by car to rendezvous points, please park carefully in order not to obstruct gateways or cause a danger to other road users. (Access points are places along the route where facilities and car parking space is available for the option of a shorter walk.)
- **Be prepared!** Carry a compass (all the map sections in the guide are north orientated). A pair of binoculars is useful to 'spy out' distant waymark signs. Always carry a rucksack with some warm and waterproof clothing, plenty of water, a flask of hot liquid in winter, and sun protection in the form of a hat, long-sleeved shirt and sun-screen for summer.

We trust that you will enjoy these walks but participants should be aware that all outdoor pursuits carry certain risks. The author cannot accept responsibility for damage or injury to individuals or property as a result of following the route described in this guide.

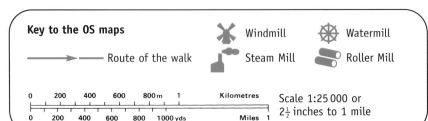

Key to the OS maps

Windmill   Watermill

Route of the walk   Steam Mill   Roller Mill

Scale 1:25 000 or 2½ inches to 1 mile

Contents

Map showing mills visted
in this book

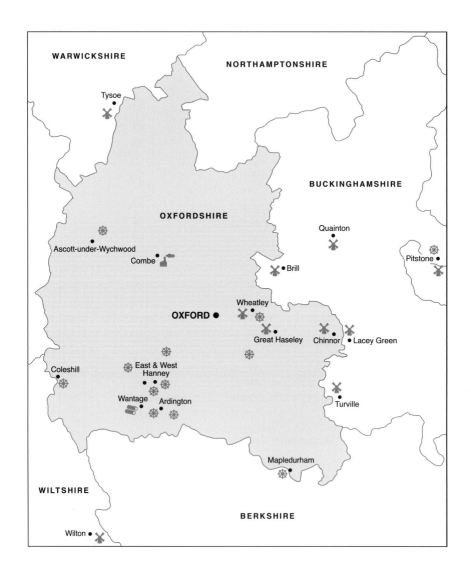

Introduction

This book describes a series of circular walks in the Oxford region, each averaging ten miles and including one or more mills. We chose the theme of mills as they are a focal point of the landscape, having been an essential part of village life. Thus they are well-served by footpaths and roads. We were attracted by the airy panoramas surrounding the windmills and the contrast of the peace of the riverside walks to watermills.

In the past these mills represented a considerable source of wealth for the royal, lay and ecclesiastical landowners who could make their tenants bring their grain to be ground into flour or meal and pay a toll for the privilege. A few mills are still at work, and are producing flour for sale or creating hydro-electricity. Others are conserved as ancient monuments. In some places groups of enthusiasts have gathered together, sought the expertise of millwrights and raised the money to restore their local mill to its former glory. Dispersed through the book are pages on the history, development and mechanics of mills and everyday idioms, such as 'Run of the mill', that demonstrate how integral milling once was to our culture.

It is not only the mills that we have drawn and described, but many of the local architectural features and points of interest in the villages and countryside we pass through. We have highlighted some of the buildings on the walks, which have interesting features that can be easily missed, and recorded some of the flowers, birds and butterflies in the country-side through which we pass. We realise that not everyone is keen to walk the full length of the walks, so we have provided access points and grid references. With the detailed information about the history and ecology we have provided, this book can also be enjoyed from an armchair.

We have chosen only a few of the mills in the Oxford region. There are many others to explore. We have enjoyed seeing the mills come to life over the last five years we have been researching the walks. Changes are continually happening in the countryside, so we welcome your comments, particularly on any changes on the route or for any revisions needed. These can then be put on: www.milestonestomillstones.co.uk

Elaine Steane

Milling-related idioms

Keep your nose to the grindstone – If set incorrectly, millstones could grind too hot and the flour would become cooked, and occasionally burst into flames. Therefore the miller kept his 'nose to the grindstone' to detect the temperature and condition of the meal.

Millstone round your neck – Millstones are very heavy and a millstone around your neck is a problem that prevents you from doing what you want to do.

Three sheets to the wind – A four-sailed windmill with only three of its sails covered in 'sheets' of canvas will turn clumsily because it is off balance. Thus, the term, borrowed from mariners, is applied to drunks.

Grist for one's mill – Grist is the corn that is brought to a mill to be ground. This idiom means useful experience bringing personal advantage.

As calm as a millpond – The calm water of a pond that was formed by damming a stream to provide a head of water to turn a mill wheel.

Put your shoulder to the wheel – When a miller had to turn a windmill into the wind, he 'put his shoulder to the wheel' by pushing the wheel at the bottom of the mill's tail pole. Some tail poles had a yoke for the miller's shoulder. Some millers used a horse. This saying is now taken to mean 'make an effort'.

Rule of thumb – To test the quality and grind of the flour, the miller would take a pinch of it between his thumb and finger. If too coarse, the flour would be ground again.

Wait your turn – When referring to the rotation of a windmill's sails, 'turn' (not 'spin') is the correct term. Farmers had to wait in line, often for days, until the windmill would 'turn' to grind his grain.

Fair to middling – The quality of ground meal would be fair, middling, or fine. To be 'fair to middling' is to be below one's best.

He'll never set the Thames on fire – It has been suggested that the origin of this expression, for someone who will never do anything exceptional, comes from 'temse', a sieve used to separate flour from bran, presumably because the man is not working fast enough to create sufficient dust.

Put through the mill – To be put through an ordeal, as corn is ground between stones.

Come to a grinding halt – If the millstones ground too close while the wind was dying, the mill would 'come to a grinding halt'. Hence meaning anything that stops both suddenly and awkwardly.

Run of the mill – The ordinary, daily grind.

The daily grind – The repetitive nature of milling led to the concept of 'the daily (same old) grind'.

Show your metal – Millstones often needed to be dressed (re-carved). When a miller hired an itinerant dresser, he could tell whether the man was experienced by noting the slivers of metal (thrown off from his carving tools) embedded in his hands. Variant of 'show your mettle'.

First come, first served – Because it could take days for a farmer to have his grist ground, the law was designed to prevent impatient customers (or those receiving special treatment from the miller) from queue jumping.

Tilting at windmills – Many people mistake the term for simply looking up at windmills, but the term 'tilting' refers to the act of charging one's lance at his opponent in jousting, as was the case in Cervantes' Don Quixote. Tilting at windmills, based on the story, means to battle an invisible or imagined enemy.

Source: Wilton Windmill Society

Ardington

Start and finish point SU425881

This is a walk exploring spring-line estate villages, starting by visiting the Ardington watermill, part of a Victorian model farm. We pass through Lockinge village to climb up to the Ridgeway on the Berkshire Downs where the history of sheep droving is still evident and the horse racing legend continues. As we return, we pass the West Hendred watermill.

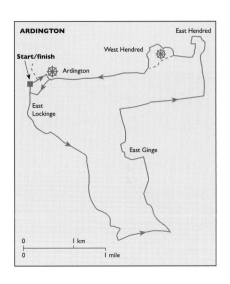

Distance: 11.0 miles (17.7 km).

Maps: Explorer 170 – Abingdon, Wantage & Vale of White Horse.
Landranger 174 – Newbury, Wantage & surrounding area.

Transport: Buses   • Thames Travel Bus 32 Wantage to Didcot. Bus stops at West and East Hendred.
           Rail   • Didcot (8 miles from route).

Taxis: Wantage   • Stuart's Taxis. Tel: 01235 770608.
                      • Supercab Taxis. Tel: 01235 770000.
                      • Webb's of Wantage. Tel: 01235 772000, mob. 07881 647777.

Car Parking: The entrance of Christopher's Wood at the west end of Ardington village SU425881 (OX12 8PD).

1

Accommodation/Public Houses/Refreshments:

Ardington
- The Boar's Head PH. Tel: 01235 835466.
- The Grocer's Chef (village stores and café). Tel: 01235 833237.

East Hendred
- Greensands B&B. Tel: 01235 833338. (0.75 miles from route).
- Eyston Arms. Tel: 01235 833320.
- The Plough Inn. Tel: 01235 833213.
- The Wheatsheaf. Tel: 01235 833229.

Wantage
- Tourist Information at Vale and Downland Museum, Church Street, Wantage. Tel: 01235 760176. www.wantage-museum.com

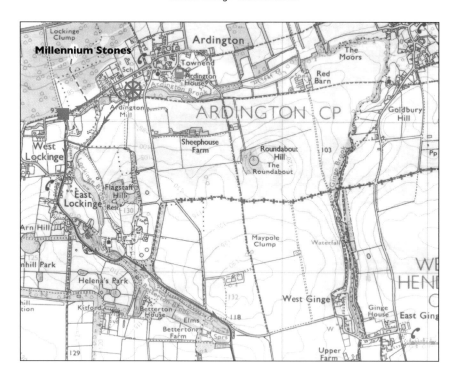

From the parking area, cross the north/south road to walk towards Ardington village for 200 yards, passing the avenue to the Millennium Stones on the left (*see p.11*). At the entrance of the Home Farm complex, bear right to follow the road beside the buildings to arrive at a small crossroads in front of the staff car park. Turn right to pass the watermill on the right.

Ardington Watermill

This mill is part of the Lockinge Estate built in the 19th century in the Victorian style of other buildings on the estate. It lost its water supply from the Ardington Brook, but then was rebuilt as a dairy, part of the progressive policy of the Lockinge Estate, which had developed a model village in East Lockinge in 1860 using what was then 'cutting edge' technology.

The mill's machinery has been restored and is now incorporated within an office development, and its sack hoist preserved. The mill wheel is still visible.

A florist workshop (www.flower-ardington.co.uk. Tel: 01235 832953 or 07767 364986) occupies the old dairy parlour and it is sometimes possible to see the remarkable Art Deco tiles that line the room. They are hand-painted Minton tiles, some featuring classical myths. You may think it is worth checking in advance to make the 1.25 mile diversion.

Minton tile

Mill opening times: by prior appointment only. Tel: Lockinge Estate office 01235 833200 (Archivist Christine Lisi, Tel: 01235 769457). National Mills weekend opening times 2–5.

Cross the Ardington Brook to turn right (SW) through a kissing gate along a footpath passing the childhood home of Hester Knight, the renowned racehorse trainer. Go through another kissing gate, across the landscaped garden to bear right along a tarmac path to the road. Here turn sharp left (S) into **East Lockinge** (this is where a shortcut from the parking area joins). Walk into the centre of the village and past the Victorian fire-engine on the left, housed in its own little half-timbered barn, and on towards Betterton and Ginge. We are now in the Victorian estate village. At the war memorial bear left to a village green. It is worth climbing the bank to see both the stone memorial to Hester Knight, made from a piece of Lower Calcareous Grit of the Corallian limestone formation, and the fine, full-sized bronze statue of Best Mate, the three-times (2002–04) Cheltenham Gold Cup winner.

Best Mate

An Estate Village
On the far side (E) of the road is parkland, part of the landscaping of the former Lockinge House. This large 18th-century house was destroyed in 1947 in order to escape double death duties. Only the large-windowed orangery survives. Similar to the situation at Chatsworth, the original cottages clustered around the church had been removed to allow the then Lockinge House more privacy. A new estate of buildings was created which still remains. An estimated 70% of the houses in both Ardington and Lockinge is still owned by the Lloyd-Lindsay family. The owners are known for their democratic way of managing the village and, for example, ensure that the village shop is maintained and that there is still a facility in the pub for locals to meet and just have a drink, rather than turning it all over to gastro-dining.

Descend from the green via some steps directly onto the road to turn right (S) past Lockinge church entrance on the left, over the Betterton Brook to gain a good view of the church and farm buildings. Ignore the two private roads on the left to pass the large wrought iron gates which were the former entrance to Betterton House. Now there is a rhino sculpture grazing! At the end of the wooded area (E) of Betterton House, turn right where the road divides (signposted Betterton) to climb the hill on a flinty track past Coldharbour Park. We continue to climb the scarp slope of the Berkshire Downs through woods to reach the Ridgeway.

On reaching the junction, on the right, under a tree, is a sarsen stone inscribed as a memorial to Penelope Betjeman, 1910–1986, who lived at Farnborough Rectory and loved to ride on the Downs.

Turn left here (E) along the wide grassy track with wide views of the Vale of White Horse below to the north and rolling Berkshire Downs to the south.

In May, the air was full of the song of skylarks and the bumblebees were hunting the ground for nest sites.

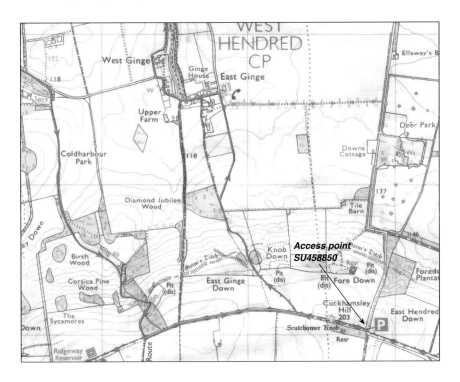

Travel for one mile passing a bridleway leaving to the left and a metal hitching post for the benefit of the many horse riders who use this route. On reaching an unmarked entrance with a high metal post and large concrete block by an iron gate, turn left (NW). For those interested in the ancient world it is worth making the 400 yard diversion to see Scutchamer Knob.

Scutchamer Knob
This mound to the south of the Ridgeway is thought to have been a Saxon royal barrow which hides the remains of, or commemorates, Cwichelm, a pagan Anglo-Saxon king who lived in the early 7th century. This barrow is very much bigger than the Bronze Age barrows or tumuli scattered over the Downs. It has been ruthlessly robbed, so that now it is hardly the conical hill that it originally was. This mound marked one of the open air 'hundred' meeting places of Berkshire representatives. A 'hundred' was an administrative area of Anglo-Saxon England.

Access Point: Scutchamer Knob car park. 4.1 miles. SU458850.

From Scutchamer Knob retrace your steps for 400 yards to bear right on a byway downhill (NW) across East Ginge Down to pass near to Grim's ditch, then through a clump of trees and down the scarp slope. Where the tracks divide take the right-hand track to arrive in the small settlement of **East Ginge**. Turn left (W) at the cycle route signed 'Wantage 4' to follow the road (W) ignoring the footpath sign to West Hendred. Instead, keep on the road over the spring of Ginge Brook, to go along the narrow lane to turn right at a small triangle of grass and take the unmarked road into **West Ginge**.

Sheep droving on the Downs
These two settlements are interesting since the old name for Ginge is Grange which would have been a barn providing shelter. It was here that the drovers broke their journey (there were two inns here), rested and washed their sheep before proceeding to the big sheep fair in East Ilsley nearly 5 miles away (SE). (40,000 sheep were gathered there.) The clear chalk stream water from both the spring and the wells in Ginge provided this water. The nearby place name of Coldharbour Park (SU 438862) reflects a common name for a place of shelter constructed by the wayside for wayfarers. Here it would have provided shelter for Welsh sheep drovers.

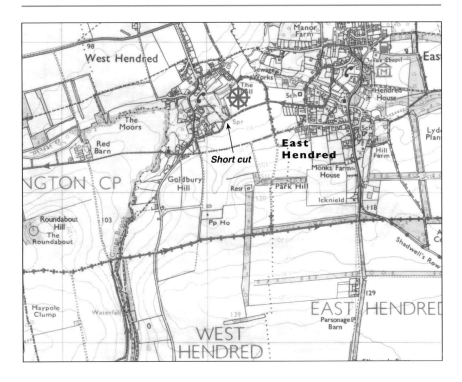

Pass the buildings of Lower Farm with its huge granges to the end of the road to turn left (N) near a tennis court onto a footpath (which is reputed to be one of the former droving routes) in the wooded valley high above the brook. Continue on past a footpath sign that descends to a bridge over the small waterfall to go along to a bigger bridge. Turn right (E) and climb the steep slope to join the byway (E) and follow this, crossing the road to West Hendred to continue beside a wood to meet the road leading left (N) to **East Hendred**. Descend the village street to arrive at a crossroads by a church on the left.

Continue (N) along the main village street passing the former village pump on the right. The Eyston Arms is to the right. Continue along the High Street to turn left at the chapel and past the Wheatsheaf pub on the right, then turn left along Orchard Lane (a reminder that this whole district was famous for apple orchards). The Plough Inn is on the left with a thatched cob wall on its boundary. At the junction with Mill Lane, turn left into Fordy Lane and left into Cat Street (there is now no evidence of the mill in East Hendred). In Cat Street turn right alongside the new cemetery.

East Hendred village, a Roman Catholic and Church of England partnership
From the crossroads the large manor house to the right is Hendred House, the family home of the Eystons. This is an ancient Catholic family and the house has a medieval hall and priesthole since it was on the escape route of the Catholic priests after the Reformation. The house includes the chapel of St Amand and St John the Baptist, first built in 1258. It fell out of use at the Reformation, was restored in 1687, but only the next year was ransacked by soldiers from William of Orange's army on their way from Hungerford to Oxford. The chapel is now back in use for religious services. Beside it, out of view, are a Roman Catholic church and primary school.

On the left is the Church of England church with its primary school beyond. The church has a rare 16th-century faceless clock, i.e. without a dial. It chimes and strikes, and plays *The Angel's Hymn* by Orlando Gibbons every three hours. There is a sundial on the south face of the tower, so you can double-check the time! David and Samantha Cameron were married here in 1996. The village also has three pubs and a shop, owned by the Eyston family.

The small medieval Champs or Jesus Chapel, now a local history museum, is open on Sunday afternoons 2.30–4.30 April–October or by appointment. Tel: 01235 833227/812796.

East Hendred church tower

Roy Jenkins, politician, author and former Chancellor of Oxford University, is buried in the new cemetery. His gravestone is a large, flat, pale stone beside the northern cemetery boundary hedge.

Follow the footpath (S), past a memorial bench to Roy Jenkins, into Church Street. On meeting the road turn right to the footpath marked 'West Hendred ½ a mile' by the side of Snells Hall. St Amand's, the house near the Hall was the former residence of Roy Jenkins. This path, which passes the Church of England primary school on the right, is

West Hendred mill

called The Furlong and is tarmac so the children from the Lockinges, Ardington and West Hendred villages can cycle safely to and from school. At a crossing of tracks 250 yards after the school, turn right in order to see the watermill on the edge of **West Hendred**.

Short cut
For a short cut, but missing the mill, continue west on The Furlong to meet the road near the church at West Hendred.

To see the mill, follow the byway to cross the Ardington Brook where there is a view to the mill and its surrounding buildings (it is on private property). Continue along Mill Lane and curve left to meet West Hendred village street. Turn left (S) through the village and start to climb up until reaching a half timbered house called Glebe House. Turn right past the church on the right, over the Ginge Brook and onto a byway crossing the fields to the west, past some farm buildings, then at the next junction continue on ignoring the path to the right to gain a good view of Ardington House, situated across the water meadows to the right.

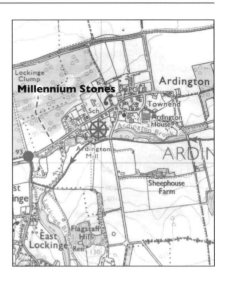

Continue on (W) along the footpath to where there is a wooden kissing gate with a path leading over the brook to the right. Here is another chance to see Ardington mill, it is only 20 yards to its site beside the brook.

Ardington House

Ardington House, built in 1720, is home of the Barings, best known for founding the famous merchant bank, the family having started as wool merchants in Exeter in the early 18th century. The house is one of the best examples of Georgian architecture in the country, famous for its imperial staircase which leads from the hall and has two matching flights leading into one at first floor level.

Open Monday–Friday 11–2 during August: also the BHs in April and May. Private tours available. Tel: 01235 821566. www.ardingtonhouse.com

Ardington Millennium Sundial and Stones SU426884

By walking 200 yards east from the parking area there is a large standing stone on the north side of the road. This is at the end of an avenue (400 yards) between woods leading to a large circular clearing. Here is a remarkable reconstructed Neolithic stone circle with fifteen standing stones and circular stones on the ground representing the solar system. At midday a flash of light is reflected down the avenue.

To complete the walk, retrace your footsteps through the kissing gate, along the footpath (SW). Go through the second kissing gate, to bear right over the brook and along a tarmac path to the road. Here turn sharp right (N) to the crossroads and parking area. There is an opportunity to visit the café and pub in the centre of Ardington village.

History

Mills have been important features of the English landscape since Roman times. They were among the first engines devised by man. Large millstones and part of a wooden watermill wheel have been found at Cawfields on Hadrian's Wall in Northumberland. The power of Haltwhistle Burn was harnessed by using an undershot wheel (the water entering at the level of the lowest paddles and turning the wheel by the horizontal impact of the fast flowing water). It has been estimated that this force could generate 1.25 horsepower which would have produced sufficient ground corn each day to feed 460 people and animals.

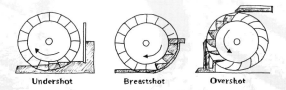

Undershot   Breastshot   Overshot

During the Anglo-Saxon period many more watermills were built: over two hundred were recorded in Domesday Book (1086) for Oxfordshire alone.

Excavations in Tamworth, Staffordshire have shown that the Anglo Saxons were already constructing leats (raised river channels) and millpools to create a force of water. This type of horizontal mill was still in use in the Orkney islands, off Scotland, into the 19th century.

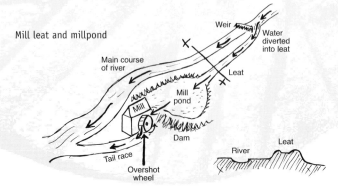

Mill leat and millpond

Weir

Water diverted into leat

Main course of river

Leat

Mill pond

Mill

Dam

Leat

River

Tail race

Overshot wheel

Ascott-under-Wychwood

Start and finish point SP299187

Our walk begins from the village to follow the quiet farmland valley of the River Evenlode. After passing the Ascott mill, we climb the opposite valley side to Chadlington where there was another watermill. We end the walk by returning along the valley side visiting Shorthampton church with its fine medieval wall paintings. Back in Ascott village, there are the remains of two Norman castles.

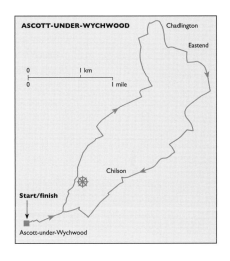

Distance:	8.3 miles (13.4 km).

Maps: Explorer OL 45 – The Cotswolds.
Explorer 180 – Oxford, Witney and Woodstock.
Explorer 191 – Banbury, Bicester and Chipping Norton.
Landranger 164 – Oxford.

Transport: Buses   • Oxford–Chipping Norton Stagecoach S3.
• Witney–Chipping Norton Stagecoach X9.
Rail   • Ascott station, Great Western Cotswold Line.

Taxis: Charlbury   • Evenlode Valley Travel. Tel: 01608 751729.
• Bobby's Taxis. Tel: 07828 158686.

Car Parking: Ascott Earl, Shipton Road (NW of the church in Ascott-under-Wychwood)
SP299187 (OX7 6DG).

Accommodation/Public Houses/Refreshments:

Ascott-under-Wychwood
- Village Shop, High Street. Tel: 01993 831240.
- The Swan Inn. Tel: 01993 832332.
  www.swanatascott.com
- Meadowbank House B&B. Tel: 01993 830612.
  www.meadowbank-ascott.co.uk
- College Farm B&B. Tel: 01993 831900.

Chadlington
- The Tite Inn. Tel: 01608 676910. www.thetiteinn.co.uk
- Chadlington Quality Foods, community shop.
  Tel: 01608 676675.
- Café de la Post. Tel: 01608 676461.
  www.cafedelapost.com
- Upper Court Farm B&B. Tel: 01608 676296.
  www.uppercourtfarm.co.uk

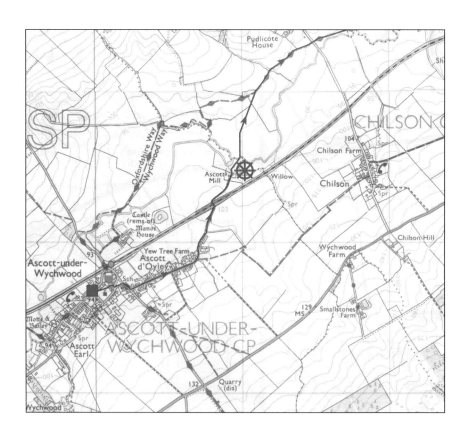

From outside The Boundary House with its round *oeil-de-boeuf* window, turn right (NE) into Church View and immediately left into the churchyard of Holy Trinity Church with its Norman features. Go along the path under the lime tree avenue to arrive in Church Close beside Forge Garage. Cross the road to the triangular village green.

Ascott Martyrs
A set of four benches around the chestnut tree in the centre of the green each bear a plaque commemorating the sixteen young women known as the 'Ascott Martyrs'. In 1873 some local men who had dared to join the new Agricultural Workers Union were sacked, so replacement workers from the village of Ramsden were hired. However, the women tried to stop these workers and to convince them to join the Union. The women were arrested, and taken to Chipping Norton where they were sentenced to 10 days imprisonment with hard labour. By 9pm that day a crowd of 1000 people had surrounded the Police Court. The local community remained furious at the treatment of the women and a personal appeal was sent to Queen Victoria who pardoned the women. She gave each of them 5 shillings and a red-flannel petticoat and the Union gave each of them £5 and enough blue silk to make a dress! More significantly, local agricultural wages were raised by more than 20%.

Turn right past the school to turn left (E) by the sign to the Village Shop into the High Street, leading to Mill Lane. Pass by the village shop on the left and a cottage with an old plough on its roof, complete with green-eyed, wrought iron cats running along it! Pass d'Oyley House on the right, with its fine stone porch since we are now in Ascott d'Oyley, named after the Norman d'Oyley family. At Yew Tree Farm, bear left (N) onto a footpath signed 'Pudlicote 1½' and follow it along the tarmac track downhill to cross the Cotswold Line to arrive at the watermill.

Ascott-under-Wychwood watermill (SP309194)

This is a three-storey mill built in 1840 that used the water from the River Evenlode to grind corn. Until the 1970s there was a weir across the river that provided water to fill the leat to the left (W) of the mill. The long dried-out grassy leat is still visible. Some of the stonework of the weir can also be seen by the river. The mill pond to the right, east of the mill, still has water in it.

All the machinery and millstones are *in situ* and now form part of a private house. By looking through the last window on the right before the gate, the wooden mill wheel is visible from the outside. It is a breastshot wheel, i.e. the water enters the buckets or strikes the paddles at axle height and passes under the wheel, but it no longer has a water supply to drive it.

Open on National Mills Weekend or contact Anne and Nigel Braithwaite, Tel: 01993 831282. ascottmill@aol.com

The breastshot wheel

From the mill follow the footpath (NE) to cross the River Evenlode via a footbridge. On the other side, do not take the path right alongside the river, but go (N, 20°) across the field aiming right of an oak tree, to turn right at the far side towards a stile in a hedge near the far right-hand corner. Having crossed the stile, bear left across the corner of the field to join a bridleway which also forms part of the Oxfordshire Way and Wychwood Way. Turn right to follow this way through a gate and across a field (NE, 60°) along a line of mostly poplar trees with a good view of Pudlicote House (Old English 'cottage in the puddle').

We saw a kestrel hunting in this field, with its young calling for their parents from a large oak tree.

Go through another gate onto a track to leave the Oxfordshire Way by turning left uphill along the lane towards Pudlicote House (200 yards).

From Pudlicote House turn right (NE), opposite two drive entrances, onto a bridleway marked 'Chadlington 1½ miles'. Walk first on the right (S) side of the hedge, then on the left (N). Follow this bridleway (NE, 58°) with its tall multi-specied hedge for nearly ¾ mile.

This hedge was laden with blackberries and hawthorn berries with the dogwood leaves a dark purple when we passed in September.

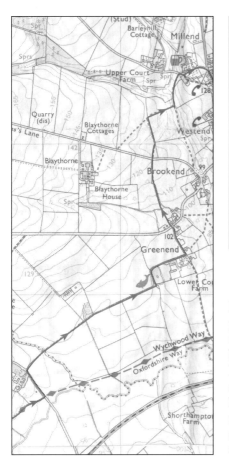

A letter box home
On the left-hand side of the drive to Pudlicote House is a GR post box with a narrow opening. In May 2014, there was an official Royal Mail notice blocking off the opening. In the typed letter of apology it was explained that collections would be suspended due to nesting birds inside the box. The Manager "hoped that people would understand the reasons for the closure, and collections would be resumed when the birds left".

Where the track divides, turn left by the former medieval fish pond of Lower Court Farm, now a fishing lake. Follow the track as it bends right to a small lane at Old Forge Cottage. There is an old tap set in the wall that supplied water before the village was connected to mains water. Turn left (N) to meet a small green and the road at Greenend.

Cross the road to continue on a footpath signed 'Millend ½ mile' to go over a stile to follow the left side of the field hedge (N), over a footbridge, and on up the next field, to make a small 'kink' by going over another footbridge into the adjacent field for 60 yards. Return through a gap in the hedge, continuing (N) along the left side of the hedge. Go through a metal kissing

> **End as a place name**
> Greenend is the first of the five 'ends' of the village — Greenend, Brookend, Millend, Westend and Eastend. The origin of 'end' here is an Old English word meaning 'district' and frequently found in former wooded areas of Oxfordshire.

gate onto another road into **Chadlington** at Brookend. Cross the lane and over a traditional Cotswold stone slab stile across the field corner (N) to walk along the hedgerow on the right for 200 yards. Halfway along the field, and where another footpath joins from the left, turn right (NE) over a stile and go down the field (E) towards the centre of the village.

Robin's Pincushion
This field is a meadow full of wildflowers, including knapweed, scabious, thistle and ragwort. We saw a Robin's pincushion on one of the wild roses. This prickly growth is caused by a female gall wasp that lays up to 60 eggs within the leaf-bud. The growth is a reaction by the plant to the eggs. 'Robin' refers to the sprite Robin Goodfellow, a name that Puck used in Shakespeare's *A Midsummer Night's Dream*.

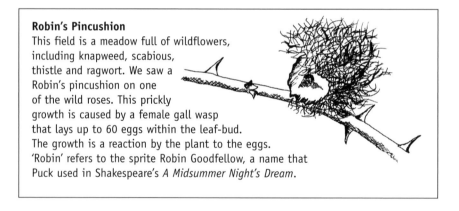

At the hedge boundary, go over the brook, turn left (not on the path uphill) through the wide wooden gate. Follow the course of the brook, but after only 100 yards there is a chance to turn left on a small path towards the brook where there is a waterfall, a stone crossing and a raised channel. This is the site of one of the mills shown in this wood on an 18th-century map. The overgrown mill leat, which used to supply water to the mills, can be seen as a raised channel on the left. Retrace your steps to rejoin the footpath (N) towards Millend. Turn right to the Tite Inn on the outskirts of the village.

The Tite Inn at Millend

The Tite Inn gets its name from the *tyte* or watering hole below the inn, a name in use since Saxon times. The water is sparklingly clear. It is used nowadays for cattle and horses, but supplied the drinking water until 1986. The landlord told us that the stream from the spring was diverted under the pub to cool the casks of beer. Previous landlords had run up and down to the cellar and filled jugs with cooled beer.

The Tite Spring, Millend

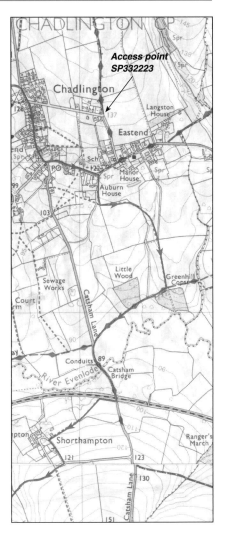

From the Tite Inn, climb the slope passing Mill House to the right and Inglenook Cottage to the left with its semi-circular bread oven protruding from the house.

The small road to the left 'The Tuer' is a local name (found elsewhere in Oxfordshire e.g. in Deddington spelt Tchure) for a narrow alley. In other parts of the country narrow ways are called ginnels or twittens.

At the road junction turn right (SE) onto the Chipping Norton Road. Continue on past the bus stop and Church Road, and along to Westend. On the right there is a lively community shop CQF (Chadlington Quality Foods).

Access Point: Chadlington (Church Road) 3.7 miles. Pub, café, B&B, shop. Car parking on Church Road by the start of Green Lane, near the Bowling Green (600 yards from route). SP332223.

At Harvey's Corner (named after an elderly man who lived in the crossroads cottage for many years), there is the former post office, now the Café de la Post. Turn left (E) along Chapel Road, signposted 'Dean and Spelsbury'. Pass the large farmhouse, 'Ploughshares', on the right ignoring the first footpath sign to the right, but at a bend in the road after Grove Cottage, turn right (S) at a sign 'Charlbury 2½' in front of a stone wall.

St Nicholas' Church, Chadlington
Here is a 200-yard optional diversion along the road to see the Manor House and the church at the Eastend part of the village. Pass Chadlington House, formerly the Parsonage, with its fleur-de-lys and barley-sugar iron railings, to the left. St Nicholas' Church is beyond the large Manor House on the right. It is Norman in origin, but has been refurbished through the centuries. Of particular interest is the 'Green Man' head carved high up on the external buttress of the NE corner of the church. (See also the 'green man' in the Pitstone windmill walk). The Chadlington 'green man' is unusual because normally trees grow down from the face to form a beard, but here the trunk forms the nose and the branches are the eyebrows. Even more unusual is the similar carved head in the same position of the south wall, though it is doubted that this is a true 'green man' (*source, church guide, 2013*).

Green Man, St Nicholas' Church, Chadlington

Returning to the route, go down a track (S) that is known locally as Watery Lane since there is spring water feeding a trough on the left.

The water looked so clear that, after a local person said that she drank it all the time, we tasted the sweet water.

Pass Auburn House, ignoring a footpath leaving on the right, to go through the gap in the trees into the open field beyond. Turn left (E) to walk along the field edge, with good views of the Manor House with its Cedar of Lebanon on the left. At a culvert, turn left over a stile beside a wide green-painted metal gate, to then turn right downhill on the right side of a field to a second green gate. Go over a brook and keep right to a third green gate and stile. On the track on the other side turn right (S) descending the slope of the river valley to the partly coniferous Greenhill Copse. At the wood turn right (SW) to follow the path beside the hedgerow which is part of the Wychwood Way. Pass Little Wood on the right. On meeting Catsham Lane, turn left (S) taking great care of the traffic, to cross the River Evenlode bridge, and 200 yards further on to the railway bridge. Immediately after this bridge, turn right (W) through a wooden kissing gate signed 'Shorthampton ¼' and go along the left side of a hedge for 150 yards. Here, bear left uphill along a grassy hollow way in between the remains of the medieval ridge and furrow ploughing. The bellcote of Shorthampton Church with its yew trees can be seen on the hill above. Go through a gap in the hedge in the far right corner of the field to follow the right side of a stone wall, passing left of a cowshed and its enclosure.

We noticed a spring on this hillside with willow trees growing. This is one of the springs of the spring-line where the water emerges from the porous limestone when it meets the impervious clay soil of the valley side.

At the field corner, go through the wooden kissing gate and turn left uphill towards Shorthampton Church.

Shorthampton Church

This small, simple church, originally Norman, has impressive 13th-century wall paintings. The splayed window in the north wall opposite the door is outlined in red to give the illusion of cut stone. The Doom or Last Judgement is one of the exceptional medieval wall paintings which include St George and the Dragon. The box pews remain and there is a 15th-century squint, a narrow, slanted window, which allowed people whose view was blocked to see the priest at the altar.

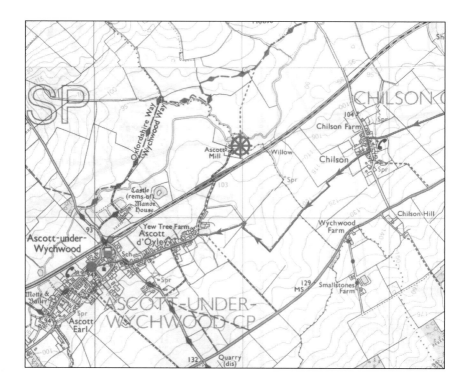

From the church, turn right uphill and right again (SW) to where the lane turns downhill. Here, continue ahead (SW) to join a bridleway, parallel to the river valley. Keep right of the hedge, then between hedges, past a bench and over a brook, to arrive in the village of **Chilson**. This village is also, like Chadlington, sited on the spring-line, where the water comes to the surface, so ensuring a constant water supply to earlier inhabitants. Turn left uphill (SE) for only 60 yards, to The Old Beer House on the left, to turn right (SW) on a bridleway along School Lane. Go through a small gate on the left to follow the left side of a hedge in the same direction (SW) through two fields. At a narrow hedge gap, before a large field, turn left for 50 yards up to the hedgerow and turn right to follow the hedge (SW) for two more fields, turning right again around the far end of the second field. Here turn right yet again (NE) for only 30 yards, to turn left through a narrow hedge gap to go sharp left on the bridleway (SW) towards the buildings of Yew Tree Farm on the edge of Ascott-under-Wychwood.

We are now in Ascott d'Oyley, with d'Oyley House on the left. Robert d'Oyley was given extensive lands by William the Conqueror. He was the first Norman overlord of Oxford, and developed the castle and built Grandpont, the bridge over the Thames, still in use, which replaced the old oxen ford.

Turn left into the High Street to retrace your steps back to the village. At the green, bear right into Church Close and back to Shipton Road, the bus stop and parking area.

Norman Castles – d'Oyley Castle and Ascott Earl Castle.

A most remarkable pair of castles lie within a few hundred yards of each other within the village of Ascott-under-Wychwood. One is of motte and bailey form, while excavations established that the other one had a stone tower from the outset with clay mounded up around its base. The first one is now a 16th century manor house (SP302190) which is worth a short diversion. (Go over the railway bridge in the village and along the road for 80 yards (NW) and then right for 200 yards along the Oxfordshire Way). The house stands within the bailey (an enclosure) of the former Norman castle of Ascott d'Oyley built in 1129, but demolished by 1175. Behind the farmhouse is the motte (mound) with trees on it where the castle once stood and is clearly visible. The manor house is a remarkable building in itself with a 17th-century barn with a columbarium (dovecote) in the gable, and a brick and half timber granary on staddle stones. We particularly liked the wooden-turreted, castle-like treehouse in the garden. In Ascott Earl, just beyond the parking area, are turf mounds marking the site of another Norman motte and bailey castle built on the site of an Iron Age settlement. These can be seen from the bridge over the River Evenlode on the footpath in the south-west corner of the village.

Post Mills

During the 12th century water mills were supplemented by windmills which were built on hill tops or on flat ground where there was plenty of wind. The earliest type was the post mill where the body of the mill containing the machinery revolved around a massive post. Because the post allowed a rotary action, the mill could be turned so that its sails faced the wind (*see Pitstone windmill, p.117*).

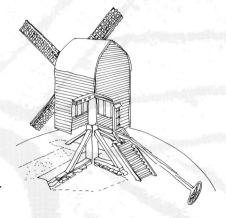

The post mill was one of the outstanding achievements of the medieval carpenter. It consisted of a small timber-framed building designed to pivot on a single vertical support. This massive central post was set on a pair of oaken cross-trees buried in the ground with the earth heaped round them for greater stability. These windmill mounds often remain in the landscape long after the disappearance of the mill itself, and are not to be confused with barrow mounds. These mounds often had a central depression where the timbers were buried. The frame of the mill was carefully assembled using mortice and tenon joints held together by trenails (wooden pegs). From the 18th century post mills were frequently provided with a round house (*see Brill walk, p.25*), a circular enclosure of brick or stone round the base and used by the miller for storage.

Brill

Start and finish point SP652142

We set off from the windmill on the hilltop site of Edward the Confessor's former royal hunting lodge in the centre of Bernwood Forest. We then descend to the lower ground where the gracious Wotton House and its Capability Brown parkland are sited. The walk takes us to a rare vernacular building survival, a thatched hovel, in the village of Ludgershall, and back over Oxfordshire's Muswell Hill.

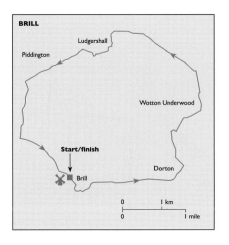

Distance: 9.5 miles (15.3 km).

Maps: Explorer 180 – Oxford, Witney and Woodstock.
Landranger 164 – Oxford and surrounding area.

Transport: Bus   • Heyfordian Travel 118 from Oxford to Thame.
Tel: 01869 241500.

Taxis: Thame   • A2B Taxis. Tel: 01844 208125.
Bicester   • Alpha Cars. Tel: 01869 252552/323236.
Oxford   • Radio ABC Taxis. Tel: 01865 242424.

Car Parking: Brill Windmill car park. SP652142 (HP18 9TG).

Accommodation/Public Houses/Refreshments:
Ludgershall   • The Bull and Butcher PH. Tel: 01844 238094.
www.bullandbutcher.co.uk
Brill   • The Pheasant PH, B&B, Windmill Street.
Tel: 01844 239370. www.thepheasant.co.uk

- The Pointer PH, Church Street. Tel: 01844 238339.
www.thepointerbrill.com
- Brill Parish Church. Cream teas. 3–5pm (weekends only)
July–September.
- Poletrees Farm B&B. Tel: 01844 238276.
(1.25 miles N of Brill).

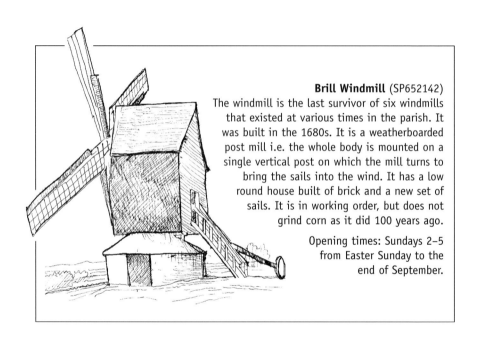

Brill Windmill (SP652142)
The windmill is the last survivor of six windmills that existed at various times in the parish. It was built in the 1680s. It is a weatherboarded post mill i.e. the whole body is mounted on a single vertical post on which the mill turns to bring the sails into the wind. It has a low round house built of brick and a new set of sails. It is in working order, but does not grind corn as it did 100 years ago.

Opening times: Sundays 2–5 from Easter Sunday to the end of September.

Brill and its Geology
At 613 feet altitude, Brill is an outlier hill which is capped by harder sandstone resistant to erosion. The underlying clays around the hill have been eroded to form the low clay vales characteristic of this part of Buckinghamshire. The Whitchurch sandstone produces the distinct red, iron-rich colour seen in the walls and buildings of Brill. The area around the windmill is pock-marked with small clay pits. Further down the hill The Kiln House is passed near the end of the walk, where the Kimmeridge Clay has been exploited for brick making, with evidence for kilns going back to the 13th century.

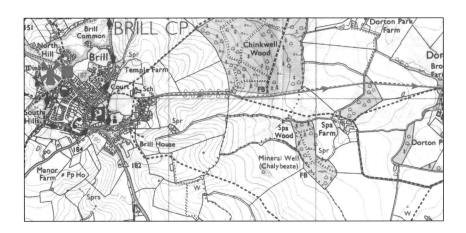

Set off from the car park (SE) to pass The Pheasant Inn on the right, then the Old Coach House on the right and the Old Bakery on the left. The small road to the right, Brae Hill, refers to the original British place name, meaning a 'hill'. *Bre* (British) + Old English 'hyll' becomes Brill. At the road junction, turn right (S) into the High Street.

There is a good mixture of brick-built houses with, on the left, No. 11, High Street with its fine oak studded door, and an 18th century Sun Fire Insurance badge. In those days, if there was no sign indicating that you had paid insurance, the fire brigade would not put out the fire. On the right is the tall United Reformed Church with a barometer in the wall nearby, erected to the memory of Sir Edmund Verney Bart of Claydon House (see Quainton windmill walk, page 129).

Keep left at the first triangular green, passing the Old Post Office to enter Church Street. Go past The Pointer pub on the left and turn left again across The Green. On reaching a road, called The Firs, go down it until the tarmac ends at No. 35. Here go left onto an unmarked gravel track. Descend this to go right to the gate. (NB when we walked through there was a 'Beware of the Bull' sign but no bull in the field and the path seemed to be well used.) Go through the metal gate and descend the hill (E) aiming for the edge of Chinkwell Wood below. The hard sandstone forms this steep slope with a view to Parkpale Farm to the right (SE) and the gables of Ashfold School (E) at Dorton below.

The name Parkpale refers to the original deer fence around the medieval hunting estate. These pales were cunningly designed so that wild deer could get in to the wood but could not jump out again.

Go through another gate to continue descending, keeping close to the edge of the wood (beware of diverging onto the more south-easterly path). At the corner of the wood cross a stile, then 25 yards on, at the corner of the field, bear half right, cross the middle of the field aiming for the right-hand side of the brow of the hill where the village of Ashendon is sited (E). Go over a stile to cross the corner of a small wood, continuing (E) to go through the corner of another smaller wood then follow the right side of the field with the barbed wire fence on your right, towards the school gables (E). Pass a pond (marked on the map) and go on towards the far telegraph pole to cross a stile to meet the path joining from Spa Farm. Go into the wood (E) and follow a narrow asphalted track near the school.

Enter the hamlet of **Dorton** where there is a brook on the left and to the right are the beautiful medieval buildings of the former Dorton House, now Ashfold School. The tall main house is built of pale red, small, medieval bricks with high boundary walls. To the left are the buildings of Brook Farm Barns including a small square weatherboarded granary on staddle stones. To the right over the wall, is a small house where the medieval bricks have been used to decorate the house, with diamond-shaped lozenge work in glazed brick to make the pattern. There are tiny windows under the eaves.

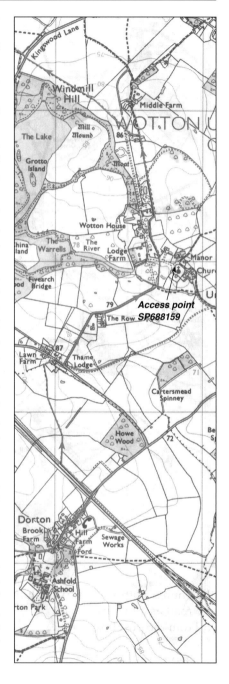

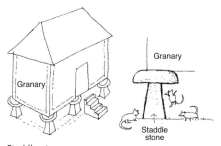

Staddle stones
These were placed to raise granaries above vermin

Brick Tax
The Brick Tax was implemented in 1784 making people pay tax on every hundred bricks that were used. As soon as this tax was passed people avoided the extra cost by trebling the size of bricks and so saving a third of their brick bill!

On joining a road, bear left to continue (NE) through the hamlet where there are some attractive hooped metal railings around the house on the right. Butts Cottage on the left, alludes to the medieval archery tradition. Every village was required to provide an area for practice (*see Wheatley walk, p.185*).

Leave the village, cross the railway bridge and go immediately left onto a footpath beside it to its end. Go over a stile to follow the right-hand hedgerow of the field (N) to cross the next stile at SP680149, to branch slightly left (NW, 345°) across the open field to a stile and waymark halfway along in the far hedge. Cross this stile and again bear slightly left (N, 356°) to another stile near a wide metal gate in front of the tall trees near Lawn Farm. Cross this stile to turn right then left along a fenced way to the minor road. Here dogleg right and left at Thame Lodge onto a minor road marked 'Wotton only'. This leads to **Wotton Underwood**. At the right-hand bend in the road is Forge Cottage (1690), a delightful brick timbered cottage with decorative barge boards in the end eaves (only visible in the winter months). The owner told us that it is the oldest house in the village, and was previously the forge. Our first view of Wotton House, with its large chimney stacks, can be seen in the distance to the left (NE). Follow the road under the avenue of standard oak trees in the hedges, keeping to the road at the left turn and beside an avenue of lime trees. At a red post box, turn right along the road leading to the church for only 50 yards to a crossing footpath. (For a short diversion of 150 yards to the church with its unusual columbarium *[see box, p.31]*, continue along the road east to the church.)

From the post box, turn left (N) onto a concreted path, through a small gate beside a large metal gate. This footpath leads along the garden hedge to a beautiful view of Wotton House.

Wotton House

This impressive example of an English Baroque house was built by the Grenville family in 1714 imitating, like many other houses of the time, Buckingham House (later Buckingham Palace) in London. It is the 'sister-house' to Stowe House, also in Buckinghamshire. The East Front, seen from the footpath, is composed of eleven bays, with giant Corinthian pilasters (again similar to Buckingham Palace). On the parapet, there are fine early 18th century stone urns and figures. As Pevsner says, "The crowning feature is a boldly regular row of rectangular chimney stacks". The two separate Queen Anne buildings, which survived a fire in the main house in 1820, are the North (right) and South (left) Pavilions, formerly the kitchens and coach house. The South Pavilion, the former home of Sir John Gielgud, is currently owned by Tony and Cherie Blair (*NB For security reasons, please do not photograph the South Pavilion*). Wotton House and its pavilions are bounded by a beautiful wrought iron screen and gates.

Wotton House and the North Pavilion

The pleasure grounds were designed by Capability Brown after he started his career at Stowe, and consist of large lakes with a serpentine canal, a Chinese bridge, a Turkish kiosk and Tuscan temples. On the highest point is a mill mound marking a post mill that stood here in the 17th century.

Only the grounds are open to the public, Wednesdays 2–5, April–early September, Admission £6, but well worth a visit. Tel: 01844 238363 for details of guided tours giving the history of the grounds. www.stately-homes.com/wotton-house

Columbarium, All Saints Church, Wotton Underwood

All Saints Church has, in the aisled family chapel, a remarkable columbarium (from the Latin for a dovecote). This is a large shelved and niched structure designed to care for multiple burials and houses twenty nine members of the Grenville family, including many of the Dukes of Buckingham.

Access Point: Wotton Underwood church. 3.6 miles. SP688159.

Continue along the footpath (N), then just past a small wooden gate is a garden gate to the house called 'The Old Post'.

In the garden of this house there is a sign for the Station Master at the station of the model railway. This railway is a reminder that the Brill Tramway, a private six-mile-long, horse-drawn route, which was built to transport goods from Wotton House to Quainton, was developed for rail passenger use in 1872. For more details see 'A Walk along the Brill Tramway' online.

The view on the right (NE), is of the Vale of Aylesbury with the hills of Quainton (*see p.129*), and Waddesdon. The radio mast on the hill above Quainton can be identified, with the tower of Quainton windmill visible just above the line of village roofs (NE, 54°). Further on, near a dead antlered oak tree with an owl box on it, is a level crossing of the model railway. The path leads to two cottages.

Just beyond the cottages (built in 1887), leave the concreted track through a kissing gate to bear left (NW, 302°) through a low gate to another kissing gate across a lane, then head towards a wood (NW). The view through the trees to the left is of the Wotton House parkland where the mill mound marked on the OS map is located — it is possible to see the large earthen mound. Go through a wooden gate and continue (NW) across Windmill Hill in a gentle descent, following the left (W) field boundary, aiming for the telegraph pole in the far hedge where there is

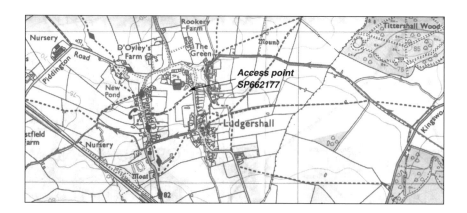

a stile. Cross the stile and over the road, crossing it with great care due to the sharp bend to the right obscuring oncoming traffic. Continue on the bridleway (NW) through a field alongside a wire fence (disregarding a footbridge and waymark signs) to reach a gate and cross another field. The views left (W) are to Muswell and Arncott Hills. Brill windmill can also be seen. Go through another field and through the next wooden gate which leads into an enclosed green lane, ignoring the footpath to the left. In the field on the right (N), and marked on the map, is a large mound, the remnants of an early post mill. These were often raised into the wind on such mounds. Go along the track to arrive at the village of **Ludgershall**. On the opposite side of the green is the Bull and Butcher pub, but to follow the route, turn left down Duck Lane. This is a low-lying area and there are brooks in the village.

The Hovel

A rare example of a surviving hovel
Just past a play area in Duck Lane is a view of a low thatched roof. The cottage on the right (private property), reached by a bridge over a small brook, is called 'The Hovel'. The definition of a hovel is 'a shed used as a human habitation, a rude or miserable dwelling place, a wretched cabin' (*Oxford English Dictionary*). This cottage, however, although having painted cob walls (i.e. made of the local mud, chopped straw and dung) and only a few very small windows, looks a very cosy home.

Ludgershall Church

The church at Ludgershall is well worth a visit. There is a Norman font dating from 1120 in the 'Aylesbury style' (meaning that the fluting and foliage are incised on the lower part of the bowl) and pillars with stone capitals bearing carvings of 14th-century men in hoods and women in wimples all interlocking arms, and a splendid hammerbeam roof with angels.

Stone capitals, Ludgershall Church

Access Point: Ludgershall Green. 5.9 miles. Pub SP662177.

After 100 yards, at a gate pillar past a house called 'Chimneys', turn right at a waymark post into a narrow footpath enclosed by a fence. When the fenced path ends after 50 yards, bear right (W) across a garden to a small metal gate. Turn right though a second metal gate and a small garden gate to walk beside a house drive. Turn left along the road, then right into Church Lane. At the end of the lane the church is to the left.

Leave the churchyard via a small gate west of the church. Cross the road to turn right and almost immediately left (W) over a stile and onto a footpath heading north-west into an oblong field. We are now on part of the route of *The Seven Shires Way*, a 234-mile long distance walk around the Oxfordshire county boundary www.sevenshiresway.co.uk. Walk in a westerly direction to the right-hand end of the far hedge where there is a stile and bridge over a brook. Turn sharp left after the brook (235°) across the next field following the right side of a ditch to a stile in a hedge. (The wetland on the left is where snipe feed, according to a local resident.) Part of this stile is made of a Great Western Railway broad gauge rail and dated 1908. Continue along this path across the Marylebone/Princes Risborough/Bicester/Birmingham railway, with great care. Continue walking (SW) along the north side of the hedge.

In winter, the remains of the headlands are just visible: mounds of soil, scraped off the medieval ploughs as they were lifted at the end of each furrow, now covered in grass.

Go over another stile into the next field.

Here the ridges and furrows are much closer together and end before the hedge, and the headlands are clearly visible. This could be a much later feature, probably made by Victorian steam ploughs.

Cross the field diagonally (SW). The next hedge, with the double stile and footbridge, is the county boundary. Crossing from Buckinghamshire into Oxfordshire, continue parallel along the right-hand side of the hedge (246°) beside a long field and ignoring the waymark sign to the left just before the brook. Cross a footbridge to turn right following the right-hand perimeter of the field and the route of the Seven Shires Way.

In winter this field is a remarkable example of medieval ridge and furrow with very pronounced reversed 'S' bends. We noticed how wide and curving the pattern was in comparison to the Victorian example we had just passed.

To the right, over the hedge, buildings on the edge of the village of Piddington are visible. On reaching the wide steel gate with a smaller gate to the right, do not cross through, but instead turn sharp left (162°) and climb the slope now walking in a south-easterly direction. Aim well to the left of the summit of Muswell Hill

The formation of the reversed 'S' bends in medieval ploughing

The shape of the ridge and furrow is determined firstly, by the length that the eight-oxen plough team could reach before needing a rest (220 yards), and secondly by the width (11 yards) imposed by the restrictions of the half-acre strips within the open field system. The reversed S-bend or wave-like pattern was produced by the ploughman who needed to begin to turn his somewhat cumbersome team well before reaching the headland at the end of the strip. The ridges and furrows are gradually formed over time by the soil being shifted by the plough up the slope of the infant ridge, and of digging further into the furrow.

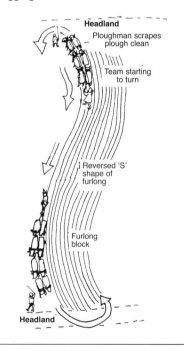

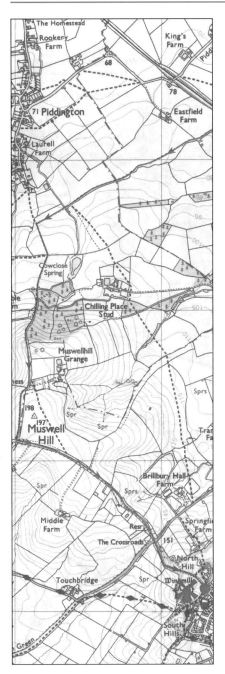

above, not along the hedge but towards the left of two willow trees in the top hedge of this field. On reaching the hedge, a waymark becomes visible. A double gate leads to the next field. Follow the hedge (S) on your left up towards Muswell Hill. Continue up through two small fields and over the stiles. Join an asphalt track for 50 yards before continuing (S) uphill on the waymarked path. On the left is an ancient hedge and ditch and the group of ash trees at the summit is called The Wilderness. Ignore the first footpath sign to the left and continue up beside the trees to a gate with an Oxfordshire waymark sign. Turn right onto the asphalted drive of Muswell Hill Grange and follow it south. This is again the county boundary with Buckinghamshire to the right (W) and Oxfordshire to the left (E). The boundary is sited here because, in the 10th and 11th centuries, the summit of Muswell Hill would have been a clear landmark for boundary making. There are extensive views to the north.

Follow the drive to turn left (E) at the road, and follow it gently downhill taking care of the traffic.

When we walked this in January there were straw-coloured hazel catkins and bright lime-coloured fungi shining on the hawthorn branches in the hedgerows. There are good views eastwards to the Vale of Aylesbury.

Keep straight on at The Crossroads and climb the hill towards **Brill**. Bear right off the road to cross the earth mounds and holes of the former quarried surface, towards the windmill.

Hartwell's Barn and Saunders Field
To the right (W) of the windmill is an interesting diversion to the education centre. The noticeboard explains some of the local brick kiln history, for example, the clay was used in medieval times to make the high-quality, glazed and lavishly decorated Brill Ware.
Saunders Field was originally part of the royal hunting forest of Bernwood where Edward the Confessor had a hunting lodge.

Brill Ware

In 1632, Brill Common was given to the people of Brill in compensation for their loss of forest rights. These rights include pannage, that is the right to graze your pigs in the forest; and bote, the right to collect firewood and the herbs and fruits of the forest.

Open weekends Easter–September. www.brill.uk.net

Leaflets about the history of Brill are in the village shop in Windmill Street.

The Great Train Robbery Hide-out
Just over a mile away, to the south of the village, lies Leatherslade Farm (SP623124) near Oakley, which was the hide-out of the 15-strong gang of the Great Train Robbery (1963), committed near Leighton Buzzard, 23 miles away (*see Pitstone walk, p.117*). A public footpath goes by the farm.

Chinnor

Start and finish point SP757010

Starting from the village of Chinnor we climb through the beech woods of the Chiltern Hills scarp slope. From the top there are good views across south Oxfordshire. We descend to reach the ancient Upper and Lower Icknield Ways crossing the land below. On arriving back at Chinnor, the restored windmill can be visited.

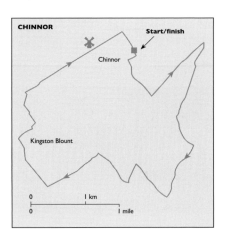

Distance: 8.3 miles (13.4 km)

Maps: Explorer 171 – Chiltern Hills West, Henley-on-Thames and Wallingford.
Explorer 181 – Chiltern Hills North.
Landranger 164 – Oxford.

Transport: Buses   • Chinnor Arriva 40 (Mon–Sat).
Tel: Traveline 08713 002233.
• Carousel link40 (Mon–Sat).
Tel: 01494 450151. www.carouselbuses.co.uk

Taxis: Chinnor   • Chinnor Cabs. Tel: 01844 353637.
• RCR Private Hire. Tel: 01844 354334.

Car Parking: Chinnor High Street car park SP757010 (OX39 4DH).

Accommodation/Public Houses/Refreshments:
Kingston Blount   • The Cherry Tree Inn, B&B. Tel: 01844 355966.
www.cherrytreekingstonblount.co.uk
• Town Farm Cottage (self catering). Tel: 01844 352152.
www.townfarmcottage.co.uk

37

Chinnor

- The Crown PH. Tel: 01844 351244.
  www.thecrownchinnor.co.uk.
- The Red Lion Inn. Tel: 01844 353468.
  www.redlioninchinnor.co.uk
- The Village Centre, High Street (restaurant/
  coffee shop/toilets). Tel: 01844 353733.
  Open Mon–Fri, 8.30–5.00 and Sat, 8.30–2.30.
- Chinnor & Princes Risborough Railway buffet.
  Tel: 01844 353535. www.chinnorrailway.co.uk

Crowell

- The Shepherd's Crook PH. Tel: 01844 355266.
  (0.5 miles from the route)

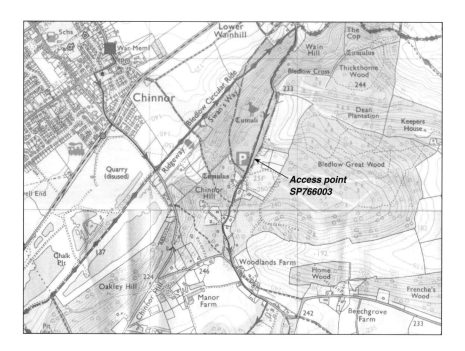

From the High Street car park turn right (SE) and right again at the
Spar shop into Church Road. Pass the church to turn left into Church
Lane to join Hill Road. Start climbing the hill and go over the bridge of
the Chinnor and Princes Risborough steam railway. At the roundabout
with the road leading to the station, there is an optional 150 yard diversion to the station where there is a buffet available in the old railway
carriages.

Buffet car

Chinnor and Princes Risborough Railway
This is a heritage steam railway that runs along the base of the Chiltern Hills, with its only station at Chinnor. As we walked we could spot the brown and cream carriages and hear the nostalgic whistle of the steam engine.

Talking Timetable, Tel: 01844 353535.

www.chinnorrailway.co.uk

Continue to climb the hill, then at the end of the footway, on the opposite side of the road is a wooden set of stairs. Cross the road with care, climb the steps and enter the playing field. If there is no game on, cross diagonally left (SE) to the far side. Go through the hedge gap to turn left onto the Ridgeway.

The Ridgeway, its history and its natural history
The Ridgeway, a prehistoric track, starts from
Ivinghoe Beacon (*see Pitstone walk, p.117*) before
crossing the River Thames at Goring and traversing
the Berkshire Downs to Avebury in Wiltshire.
The chalky soil produces a mixture of rare
chalk grassland, scrub and woodland.
A single square metre of chalk turf may contain
between thirty and forty separate plant species.
These include: bee orchid, Chiltern gentian,
birdsfoot trefoil, wild candytuft and gorse.

Chiltern gentian

These plants also attract a variety of butterflies,
such as marbled white and comma. The birds of
prey now include red kites as well as kestrels,
sparrowhawks and buzzards.

Comma butterfly   *Source: The Wildlife Trust.*

Follow this broad, straight path along the bottom of the scarp slope
with south Oxfordshire and the village of Chinnor to the left (N). Ignore
a footpath leading to the right, to continue along the track, then 250 yards
after passing a house called 'Greenway', enter the 'Wildlife Walk'
gateway on the right. It is possible to walk through this Chinnor Hill
nature reserve which runs parallel to the Ridgeway path, and worth
the short diversion in summer to see a variety of orchids in the chalk
grassland. Leave the nature reserve by exiting through the metal gate
and down steps back onto the track and turn right to continue on the
Ridgeway (NE). Ignore a crossing bridleway 100 yards further on, to
reach the houses of **Hempton Wainhill**. At a waymark signed 'Chinnor
Reserve and Barrows' turn sharp right to start a steep ascent of a sunken
way. Keep alongside a wire fence, then just after the Chalk Pits information board, go through a small wooden kissing gate on the right and into
the woods on a permissive path keeping to the contours of the hill, still in
the same direction (SW).

Chalk Pits

This slope, as the notice tells us, is another part of the BBOWT's nature reserve. This open ground is dotted with chalk pits which were originally dug by local farmers. They used the chalk to lime the more acid clay fields found at the base of the Chilterns. The pits now create suntraps providing warm conditions in which plants and insects thrive. In August we saw peacock and gatekeeper butterflies feeding on the small scabious. Greater knapweed, common rock rose, hairy violets and kidney vetch also grow here.

Common rock rose

On emerging from the woods, there are seats and an interpretation board explaining grassland management. The magnificent view north is of south Oxfordshire. From the board turn uphill past some of the nearby juniper bushes and through a metal kissing gate. Turn right (S) along a broad wooded path which leads to the BBOWT car park.

Access point: BBOWT car park at the end of Hill Top Lane, near Bledlow Ridge 2 miles. SP766003.

From the car park, walk (SW) along Hill Top Lane, which is the county boundary between Buckinghamshire to the left (E) and Oxfordshire to the right (W), then turn left along the road (Red Lane) passing Woodlands Farm on the left. Take great care of the traffic on this road. Before passing the white-boarded house on the left, turn right at a waymark marked 'Sprig's Alley ¾', to enter the woodland (SW) and down into the valley of Sunley Wood. Continue in the same direction up the slope, (on a way-marked path – CH 31), along the bridleway on the edge of Venus Wood. Arrive at the hamlet of **Sprig's Alley** to turn right over a hidden stile near Pond Farm. Go over another stile to cross the field (NW) and then a stile to enter the wood. Leave the wood by a further stile and continue diagonally left across a large field (NW) to a wide gate and stile in the far right corner of the field. Turn left onto a minor road and follow it, ignoring the first footpath sign to the right, past houses called Yew Trees and Home Close. Turn right (NW) onto a Restricted Byway at the sharp road corner at the west end of the **Crowell Hill** settlement.

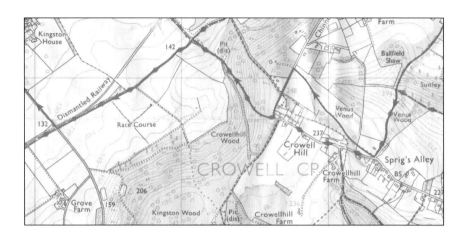

Sunken way

Transhumance

The sunken way, between coppiced hazel trees and large standard beech trees, that descends steeply down the scarp slope is a former droveway for transhumance (the seasonal movement of people and their flocks between pastures). In Anglo-Saxon times flocks of sheep and cattle, having grazed in the wood pasture, would have been driven down such tracks in winter to the settlements below.

Pigs were also included in the rights of pannage, feeding on the fallen acorns, beech mast and chestnut. Constant use over the centuries has resulted in producing these hollow ways.

Pannage   B.M. MS. Roy. 2. B, VII

When we descended in December we were delighted by the variety of reds in the fruit – the scarlet rose hips, the pinks of the spindleberry tree and the yellow-red of the bryony berries.

Continue on down the slope and out of the wood to where there are views in winter (SW) along the slope as far as Wittenham Clumps. At a junction of tracks, turn left (SW) along the Ridgeway, which is also the Upper Icknield Way.

Upper and Lower Icknield Ways

The Upper Icknield Way is a prehistoric track stretching from Wells-next-the-Sea in Norfolk to Goring-on-Thames where it crosses the Thames and becomes The Ridgeway. There are two tracks, the Upper and the Lower, in this stretch along the line of the Chiltern Hills. The Upper Icknield Way, where we are now standing, would have been an all-weather road, but with many diversions around the dry valleys. The Lower way saved time and effort, but its many fords and sloughs (bogs) limited use to summer and autumn. This route became more convenient as settlements increased and became safer from wolves and unfriendly strangers. Both the ways were used for droving flocks and as military roads from Roman times. (*Oliver Rackham, 1986*).

Follow this track for ¾ mile, to turn right over the dismantled railway and along a minor road (NW) to cross the Chinnor Road (beware of the fast traffic) into the village of **Kingston Blount**, which dates back to Domesday Book.

*(NB there is an optional diversion right (NE) along the Chinnor Road on a pavement for 100 yards to the Cherry Tree pub or a bit further to The Shepherd's Crook at **Crowell**.)*

If not making the diversion, dogleg right and left into Stert Road to follow it, passing the village green on the right. Just before Lower Farm, turn right (NE) along Brook Street then left onto a footpath leading to the right side of the village hall and playing field, passing Poor's Hillock Allotments, established in 1834. On the side of the hall is a village plan which shows Kingston Blount's original rectangular layout with the centre as paddocks (now built on) for grazing and animal shelter. Bear right (N) around the playing field to go through a gap in the far corner onto the other side of the large hedgerow. Turn left here (NW), to follow the footpath on the right side of the hedge as far as the track of the Lower Icknield Way. Turn right (NE) to walk towards Chinnor passing Middle Farm and into Mill Lane. Pass the school to arrive at the windmill beside the road.

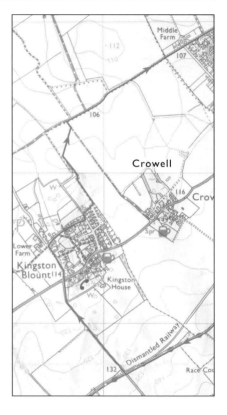

Prince Rupert and the Lower Icknield Way

Prince Rupert of the Rhine, nephew of King Charles I and commander of the Royalist cavalry during the English Civil War (1642–46), marched from Oxford along the Icknield Way with 1,200 cavalry and 800 soldiers to attack Chinnor on June 17th 1643. Fifty Parliamentarians were killed and 120 captured, arms and food pillaged, and the village set on fire.

Chinnor Windmill
(SP749010)

This post mill originally built in about 1750 has an interesting history. By 1903 it had been upgraded with all the latest technology, such as a fantail that kept it pointing into the wind and automatic 'Patent' sails sensitive to different wind strengths. However, once the miller bought a steam engine the windmill became redundant. By 1923 it was left in a state of disrepair and the site owner suddenly 'upped sticks' and left for Australia without leaving an address! Some years afterwards the parish council secured funding to rebuild the mill further down Mill Lane and the original site was bulldozed for a housing estate in 1967. The parts, including the main post, had by then been taken to Essex, but they were retrieved from a back garden and transported back to Chinnor. Some of the millstones are in the Oxfordshire County Museum and others, such as the flour grader, have been used at the Pitstone windmill in Buckinghamshire (*see Pitstone walk, p.117*).

The mill is unusual in having only three cross-trees and six piers and quarterbars. It is now the only surviving one with six 'feet', a local characteristic, since the demise of two other such mills at Bledlow Ridge and Stokenchurch. It has been restored and it is hoped it will grind flour once more.

Opening hours: Alternate Sundays 10–2.
Contact Adrian Marshall, Tel: 01844 292095, email: adrian@craftytech.co.uk

From the windmill continue along Mill Lane, passing on the right, the large, old, thatched Crossways Cottage to the junction. Cross the junction signposted Princes Risborough onto Lower Road (NE) and walk for 350 yards, taking great care of the traffic, to turn right at the Red Lion Pub into the High Street, signed 'The Village Centre'. Pass the Old Manse on the right and the striking, chequered, brick-built Manor House on the left with its old yew tree. Arrive at the village centre, car park and toilets.

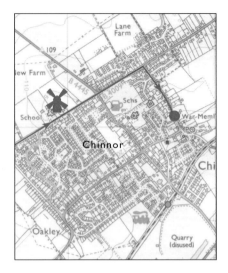

Coleshill

Start and finish point SU235935

The walk crosses the National Trust Coleshill Estate surrounding the former Coleshill House on the Oxfordshire/Wiltshire border. We visit the magnificent Great Coxwell medieval tithe barn, the Iron Age hill fort of Badbury Camp then descend to the village of Coleshill. The working watermill is on the River Cole among restored water meadows where snakeshead fritillary flowers grow in spring.

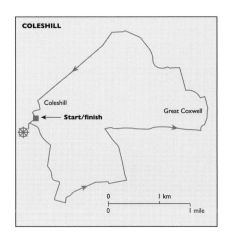

Distance: 7.6 miles (12.9 km).

Maps: Explorer 170 – Abingdon, Wantage & Vale of White Horse.
Landranger 173 – Swindon, Didcot & surrounding area.
Landranger 164 – Oxford.

Transport: Buses • Oxford–Faringdon, 66 (Great Coxwell Turn stop).
0.5 miles from Great Coxwell.
• Swindon–Highworth, 64. 2 miles from Coleshill.

Taxis: Great Coxwell • Coxwell Cars. Tel: 07772 971780.
Faringdon • Brian's Hire. Tel: 0845 2603230. www.brianshire.co.uk
Shrivenham • Academy Cars. Tel: 01793 783400.

Car Parking: In the National Trust Estate Yard, south west of the village, or if closed, in a lane nearby SU235935 (SN6 7PT).

Accommodation/Public Houses/Refreshments:
Coleshill • Radnor Arms PH. Tel: 01793 762366.
www.radnorarmscoleshill.co.uk

47

• Courtyard Community Café and Shop. 10.30–4.30 daily.
Tel: 01793 763619.

Faringdon • Tourist Information. Tel: 01367 242191.
www.visitsouthoxfordshire.co.uk

Coleshill Estate

This 7,500 acre (about 12 square miles) estate exemplifies the National Trust's specialised work in protecting the environment and working with local farmers and villagers. Coleshill House, built in the 1660s, was an outstanding example of Inigo Jones's Restoration architecture. In 1952 a fire, started by a blow lamp, destroyed the entire house. Only the gate piers on the B4019, gardens, parkland and water mill survive.

Coleshill House as it looked before it was burned down

A 'hush-hush' wartime base

During World War II the house was the High Command headquarters for the British Resistance Auxiliary Units. This was a secret network of 3,500 volunteers, who undertook intensive training in guerilla warfare in the event of a German invasion. They learned how to create an underground Operational Bases (OB). A local person told us how the volunteer men and women arrived at Swindon railway station and had to make their own way to Highworth post office. There, they gave a password to Mabel Stranks, a character rather like Miss Marple, and then were driven by truck to Coleshill House. Despite the scarcity of petrol, their journey followed a circuitous route so they would not know the exact location of the house. Winston Churchill was a frequent visitor.

Access to the park and guided walks (including World War II walks to see a replica OB) are from the National Trust office in Coleshill village, admission free, open all year.

Tel: 01793 762209. www.buscotandcoleshill@nationaltrust.org.uk

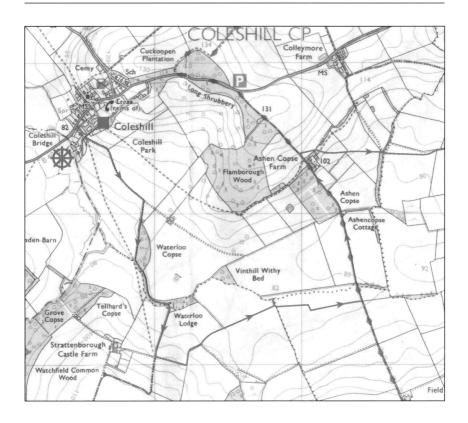

The walk starts from the National Trust Yard where there is a photographic display of the building and destruction of Coleshill House. A toilet is behind the right-hand gate. On emerging from the yard, turn right (SW) to walk down a minor road to a gateway and cattle grid into the Coleshill Park Estate.

The River Cole to the right (W) forms part of the Oxfordshire/Wiltshire county boundary. The water meadows beside it have been the centre of a major ecological restoration project which has dramatically increased the biodiversity, flood storage ability and visual appearance within a sustainable agricultural system. Wild flowers such as the snakeshead fritillary are to be found here.

Turn left (SE, 112°) along the bridleway, initially concreted. At the junction, bear right towards a small wood and pass Park Lodge on the left.

At the junction of paths, keep on the left track to continue along the inside edge of Waterloo Copse, ignoring the footpath to the right.

On looking to the right (S), a building on the hillside is unusual. It is Strattenborough Castle, which was built in 1792 to look like a mock castle and was a feature of the romantic landscaped parkland fashionable in the late 18th and early 19th centuries. When level with the building it is obvious that only the front façade was made to look like a castle, the rest being a normal farm building.

Pass Waterloo Lodge and go through the wrought-iron park gates. Turn right to climb the slope along the track towards the wind turbines to a junction of paths. Turn left (E) along a permissive bridleway (easily missed as it is not signed). Continue (E) on the left side of the hedge-row following a series of ancient boundary oak trees. Dogleg left and right, and then through a hedge gap on the right and continue following this permissive path (green footprint sign) east for nearly a mile, before joining a north/south bridleway (The D'Arcy Dalton Way). Turn left (N) along an avenue of young lime trees.

We saw cowslips and red-tailed bumble bees in the field margins, roe deer in the fields and buzzards circling above us.

Continue north past Ashencope Cottage to the right and on beside Ashen Copse on the left towards Ashen Copse Farm, brick-built with a terraced garden, on the slope above. Turn right (E) to pass left of the corrugated iron barns and right into a field by a stile. Walk diagonally across the field (E, 90°), (ignoring a signed path following the northern field boundary), to cross a double stile in the far corner and again go east across another field. Avoid a stile further to the left. At the northern end of a small wood cross the stile and footbridge, then dogleg immediately right and left along a track to then turn right along the edge of a field still travelling east. Great Coxwell church tower can be seen ahead in the distance. We have now re-joined the public right of way signs. Go through a second field, then at the end of a third field do not take a track that goes left beside a wood, but follow the field edge round to dogleg right and left over double stiles and a footbridge over a ditch.

Here we noticed young elm trees growing in the hedgerow. There are good views of the White Horse Hill and Uffington Castle to the right (S).

Continue (E) alongside the field edge and at the end of the next field, ignore a footpath over a stile to the left (N) and instead dogleg right and left round the field edge, to cross another brook via a stile into an

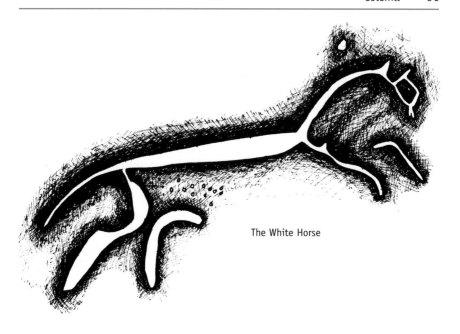

The White Horse

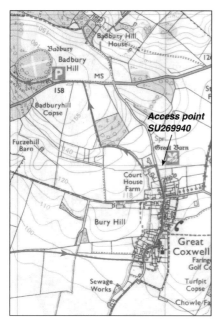

enclosed footpath to the village street of **Great Coxwell**. Turn left (N) up the village street to pass a thatched cottage on the left and a lane up to the church on the right. This leads to St Giles Church on the site of an earlier Saxon church, and which has interesting Norman features. Return to the village street to pass the handsome Chapel House.

At the road junction is Puddle-duck Lane, formerly called Coleshill Lane, an unmetalled medieval route to Coleshill in pre-turnpike days.

Continue walking along the village street in the same direction (N) to arrive at the Great Coxwell Barn on the left.

Great Coxwell Barn

This great barn is the sole surviving part of a 13th-century grange (manor) that once provided vital income to Beaulieu Abbey in Hampshire. The grange also included a windmill for grinding the grain, a pig farm and a dairy herd; cheese, butter and honey would also have been produced.

The barn itself is of monumental proportions, 144ft long and 38ft wide. William Morris described it as 'the cathedral of the working man'. The walls are of Cotswold rubble stone with a fine Stonesfield slate roof. Several slit windows are for ventilation and the small square putlog holes on the outside were where the stonemasons inserted their poles used during construction. Inside the carpentry is dated to c.1300 and oak pillars support the purlins and rafters.

Apotropaic or Witches' Marks

On the stone plinths supporting the pillars are apotropaic marks, so named from the Greek for 'turning away'. They are circles with dots in the middle, carved into the soft stone and are an ancient symbol to avert evil, and to protect against witches. They are frequently found near the entrance of buildings, windows, and fireplaces. In the stone implement shed on the left side of the entrance is a lecture area containing a useful guide to finding these apotropaic marks.

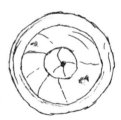

Apotropaic mark

National Trust owned, free admission, but donations welcome.

𝔍𝔄𝔦𝔳𝔟𝔦

An 18th-century graffito

Access point: Great Coxwell Barn, 4.4 miles. SU269940.

Leave the barn on the west side to cross a stile beside a metal field gate. Turn right (NW) on a path beside a field edge to then turn right (N) uphill beside the left (W) side of the wood. Here there is a spring that rises at the base of the hill.

The soil is a deep orange colour derived from the underlying Faringdon Sponge Gravel. This was formed on the sea bed in Cretaceous times (145–165 million years ago) when dinosaurs, such as Tyrannosaurus Rex, were at their most diverse stage.

Follow a path between barbed wire fences to arrive at the road. Cross the road with care and turn left (W) along the right side of the hedge following the NT path to avoid road walking. There are good views of the Thames valley to the right (N). Under the trees is Badbury Hill Iron Age hill fort car park.

Badbury Hill

Badbury Hill is one of several places that have been identified as 'Mount Badon' where King Arthur is said to have inflicted a decisive defeat on the Saxon invaders, which led to peace for a generation. It is a hilly outcrop of Lower Greensand above the Corallian Limestone ridge that runs north east towards Oxford. The hill fort, constructed about 2,500 years ago, has earthen ramparts and a ditch. It is oval in shape and would have been occupied by round huts, storage pits for grain and pens for livestock. The broadleaved trees now planted on it include beech, oak, ash, birch, hazel and wild cherry. The beech trees are thought to have been planted by WW II prisoners of war. It is worth a walk through the woods to the north side where there are fine views east to Faringdon and its folly. In spring there is a carpet of bluebells.

Access point: Badbury Hillfort NT car park 5.1 miles. SU262946

To continue the walk, go through a small gate at the far end of the car park to follow the footpath (W) past a hidden cottage. At the end of the wire garden fence, keep on the path due north ahead. Continue along this path to descend through Coxwell Wood (NW, 330°). Ignore crossing paths to emerge into the open fields and on towards Brimstone Farm. There were orangetip and brimstone butterflies feeding at the field edge.

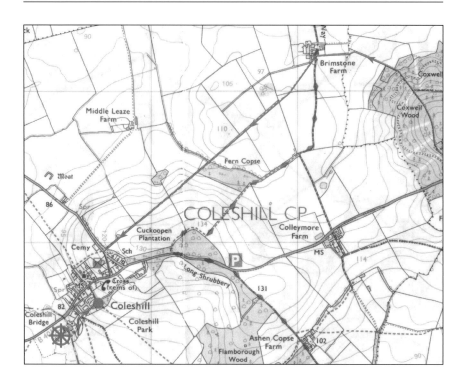

Continue to the far field boundary (NW) and dogleg left and right across a ditch and over the next field (W) to arrive at Brimstone Farm.

At Brimstone Farm do not take the track left (S) but continue through the farmyard to join a track left of the cowsheds. Take the footpath left over a stile, through the middle of a small wood to a second stile. From this stile, go diagonally right (SW, 215°) aiming across to the telegraph pole, the first to the left of the opposite field corner. Keep well left of the clump of trees. At the hedge gap and footbridge, turn right across the field corner, over the stile and along a path (SW), initially between two hedges. Continue past the end of Fern Copse over another foot-bridge and gradually climb to enjoy the wide views over the Thames Valley to the right (N). We pass a pond with an old oak tree near the top of the hill and the entry to the village of **Coleshill**. At the road, ignore the footpath sign opposite, to turn left and immediately take the right fork (S) passing the Old Forge Brewery and the Radnor Arms pub on the corner. Turn right (W) down to the village green with its remains of a medieval cross and the church up on the slope to the right.

Coleshill Church

This 15th-century church has a memorial in Coade stone, an artificial stone invented by Eleanor Coade in 1784, on the left side by the altar. It is in Gothic style, to Sir Mark Pleydell and his wife. The church has some beautiful stained-glass windows and a trefoil-headed south door to the church tower, which has gargoyles and crockets (leafy stone knobs) on the pinnacles.

Take the left (SE) minor road towards the Coleshill community shop and café, situated in some of the buildings of the former Victorian model farm.

Victorian model farm

This model farm was built in 1854, a time of relative agricultural prosperity, making use of the latest agricultural practices and technology, both in building design and in livestock management. There were even tramways which made use of the gradient for distributing the grain and manure around the buildings.

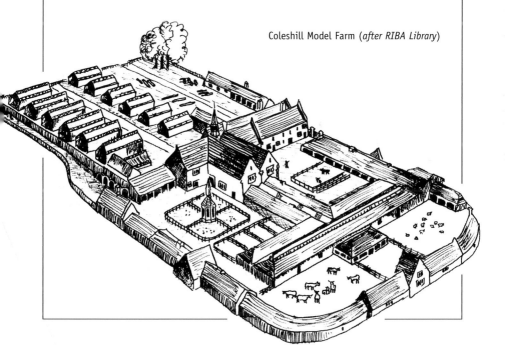

Coleshill Model Farm (*after RIBA Library*)

At the road junction, past the entry to the community café, turn right (SW) to the Estate Yard and car parking. To reach the mill, continue downhill past the entrance to the park and 100 yards down a path (SW).

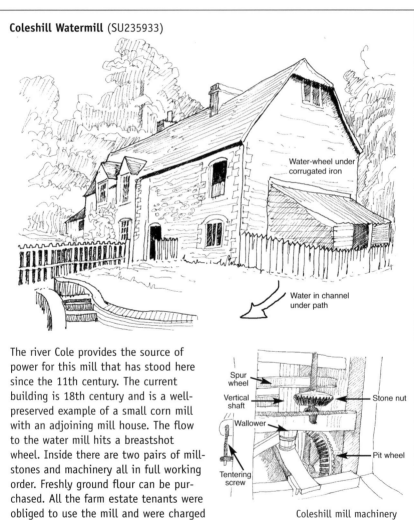

Coleshill Watermill (SU235933)

Water-wheel under corrugated iron

Water in channel under path

The river Cole provides the source of power for this mill that has stood here since the 11th century. The current building is 18th century and is a well-preserved example of a small corn mill with an adjoining mill house. The flow to the water mill hits a breastshot wheel. Inside there are two pairs of millstones and machinery all in full working order. Freshly ground flour can be purchased. All the farm estate tenants were obliged to use the mill and were charged a percentage of their ground corn.

Spur wheel
Vertical shaft
Wallower
Tentering screw
Stone nut
Pit wheel

Coleshill mill machinery

National Trust owned. Open second Sundays from April–October, 2–5. Tel: 01793 762209.

Combe

Start and finish points SP416150 or SP425158

This walk crosses the world-famous parkland of Blenheim Palace, designed by Capability Brown. We then follow the River Evenlode to Stonesfield and visit the North Leigh Roman Villa to arrive at the forest-edge settlement of East End. We walk beside the ancient woodland, with its rich flora, to arrive back at Combe mill sited by the river since Saxon times.

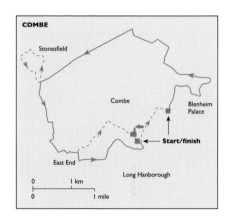

Distance: 10.8 miles (17.4 km) with circuit of Stonesfield — 9.3 miles (15 km) without.

Maps: Explorer 180 – Oxford, Witney & Woodstock.
Landranger 164 – Oxford.

Transport: Buses   • Combe, Akeman Street. Stagecoach S3 Oxford–Charlbury.
Rail   • Combe Station (only one train a day).

Taxis: Stonesfield   • Woodstock Travel. Tel: 01993 891888.
Eynsham   • Green Light Taxis. Tel: 01865 233274.
Witney   • Crescent Cars. Tel: 01899 775501.

Car Parking: Combe Steam Mill car park, SP416150 (OX29 8ET). NB on Steaming Sundays (3rd in the month) please use Combe Lodge parking, SP425158 (OX29 8ND).

Accommodation/Public Houses/Refreshments:
Stonesfield   • The White Horse Inn. Tel: 01993 608496.
www.thewhitehorseinnatstonesfield.com
East End   • Leather Bottle, B&B. Tel: 01993 882174.
• Elbie House B&B. Tel: 01993 880166.
www.cotswoldbreak.co.uk.

Combe   • Steam Mill Tea Room. Tel: 01993 358694.
             • The Cock Inn (one mile from route). Tel: 01993 891228.
               www.thecockatcombe.co.uk
             • Cream teas in the village Reading Room. Sat and Sun,
               mid July to the end of August 3–5.30.
             • Green Close B&B. Tel: 01993 891223.
               www.greenclose.net

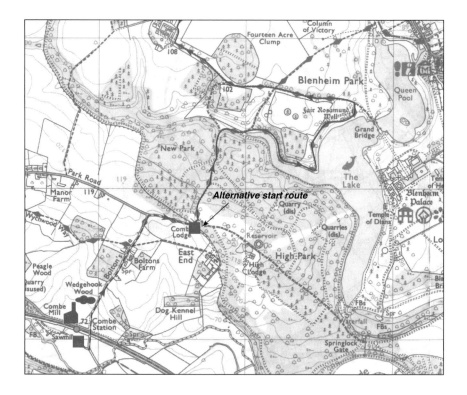

From the mill car park, turn right (E) along the entrance drive, then turn left under the railway bridge and, ignoring the road to Combe on the left, start climbing (NE) up Bolton's Lane past Bolton's Farm to a T-junction. Here, turn right at the small triangular green signposted East End towards the Combe Lodge, one of the entrances to Blenheim Park. Turn left via a kissing gate beside the large gates to enter the park, and again turn left (N, 350°) on the tarmac road.

Blenheim Park

Blenheim Park was originally a royal hunting preserve and still retains the original size and walled boundary built to contain the deer. The remains of the medieval royal residence had already been destroyed by the time the grounds were landscaped by Capability Brown and the great lake created in the 1760s. (Capability Brown was so named because he always talked about the 'capabilities' — meaning possibilities — of any landscape about which he was consulted). Blenheim Palace was built for the first Duke of Marlborough who was given the land and palace by a grateful Queen Anne as a reward for his triumphs in the War of the Spanish Succession. It is named after his victory on the field of Blenheim in Austria in 1704, which saved Europe from French domination.

We have joined the Wychwood Way, a circular walk of 29 miles around the heart of the ancient Wychwood Forest. There are old antlered oak trees on either side and an Atlas Cedar with its spreading branches; spruce and pine are further along the road on the right. Where the track curves left, bear right along the valley bottom, looking out for the huge copper beeches on the far slope. At the end of the valley bear left through a small gate then almost immediately right (E) along the stony path beside The Lake.

Atlas cedar

We saw a mallard duck with eight little ducklings, a grebe and a heron. In July there were water lilies with yellow mullein beside the track.

Continue along the lake edge, to see a vista of the Grand Bridge with the four-pinnacled Woodstock church tower beyond, and to the right, our first view of Blenheim Palace, designed by Hawksmoor and Vanbrugh. At the junction, bear right down a grassy slope to see Fair Rosamund's Well surrounded by iron railings (see following page).

Beyond Rosamund's Well, bear left climbing up the slope away from the lake to arrive at a small wooden gate onto the estate road. Although our route goes left, it is worth walking 150 yards to the right to the

Fair Rosamund

Fair Rosamund was born about 1140 and died at the age of 35. She was Henry II's mistress and legend has it that Henry kept her in the middle of a labyrinth in the original medieval Woodstock Palace to protect her from his jealous queen, Eleanor of Aquitaine. However, Eleanor used a ball of thread to find her way through the maze and forced Rosamund to drink poison. Rosamund was buried at Godstow Nunnery across the river from the Trout Inn at Godstow, near Oxford. This grave was later destroyed on the orders of the bishop, who could not tolerate the offerings of flowers at her tomb.

bridge for a good view of the Queen Pool, part of Capability Brown's landscaping. As you retrace your steps, the Column of Victory in the avenue of trees to the right (NW) can be seen. This was erected to celebrate the Duke of Marlborough's victory at Blenheim. To continue, follow the road (W) passing the crossing footpath, and go along the road between the woods. At a fork, marked Park Farm, bear right (NW) along an avenue of horse chestnut, beech and lime trees, to arrive at the front of the farm buildings. Here turn right (NE) past the buildings to the farmyard entrance. Turn right onto a footpath beside the cattle grid (NE, 22°) towards a clump of trees. Pass to the right of these trees, and

Column of Victory

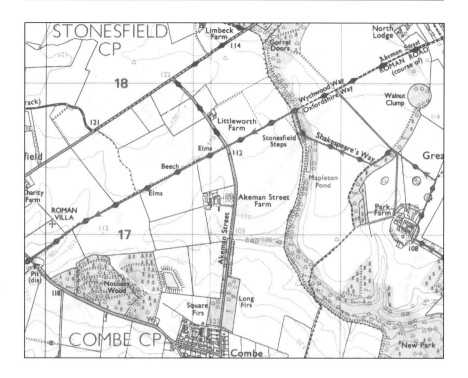

immediately after another group of copper beeches, turn left (NW, 310°) through a kissing gate and across the parkland, aiming for a gap in the belt of coniferous trees two fields ahead. Go through a kissing gate and walk across the field continuing towards the gap. At the next gate (SP423175) turn right onto the track and almost immediately left (SW) to follow the NW side of the hedgerow. At the first small gate, turn right (NW) beside the field fence. Go through a small gate and continue in the same direction to the edge of the wood for only 50 yards, before bearing left into the wood. At the broad track, turn right to walk beside the Blenheim Park boundary wall on the left. This forms part of the park pale of the original deer park. At the crossroads of tracks turn left (SW) to cross the Stonesfield Steps. Cross this ladder stile with care (it can be slippery in wet weather) to follow the route of Akeman Street, the Roman road that runs from Alchester near Bicester to Cirencester.

We have joined The Roman Way, a 174 mile walk (created by the author) on the theme of local Roman roads, and *The Shakespeare's Way* from Stratford-upon-Avon to the Globe Theatre in London.

The Structure of a Roman road
The path lies on top of the Roman agger. Agger is Latin for the raised linear mound or bank made of earth and stones on which Roman roads were built. Codrington writing in 1903 describes 'a section cut in Woodstock Park showed that the foundation of the road was of flags of the local stone called Stonesfield Slate, about an inch thick, and from 14 by 12 inches to half that wide. They were laid sloping in the direction of the road at an angle of 20° to 25° and upon this foundation was a layer of six inches of gravel under the sod. The width was 17 feet'.

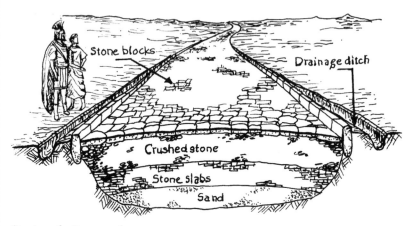

Structure of a Roman road

Continue in the same direction to cross a minor road (N–S), confusingly also called Akeman Street.

Along this part of the Roman road there are several oak and beech 'standards' (a forestry term for solitary trees grown for timber) with wild flowers on either side of the raised path, including blue scabious, yarrow, wild thyme, marjoram, knapweed and restharrow, all favouring the limestone soil.

Continue on (SW) past the site of the Stonesfield Roman villa to the right (N) although there is nothing to see now. Change to walk along the left side of the hedgerow. Cross a minor road to pass the disused Stonesfield slate mines to the right; the spoil-heaps of the unwanted waste limestone are still noticeable in the uncultivated parts of the field.

The valley of Bagg's Bottom on the left is a piece of undisturbed woodland. Its name derives from the old name for badger and the local name for a steep-sided valley.

Go through the metal kissing gate to descend along the river cliff down to the river Evenlode. Go through another kissing gate.

Alternative Route

By turning right (N) at the kissing gate, there is an optional 1.5 mile loop to Stonesfield village (see box on following page). Climb up the steep-sided path which is bordered by primroses, violets and wood anemones in spring. Where Brook Lane joins the road junction go straight ahead along Church Street, passing the High Street on the left to turn left into Pond Hill (NB bus stop on right in Woodstock Road). Follow this road passing the former Methodist Chapel on the left and the shop on the right, and descend to the small triangular green in front of the White Horse pub. (NB there is another bus stop by the green).

At the White Horse pub turn left, to follow The Ridings street (SW) into Laughton Hill.

Access Point: Stonesfield, The Ridings, E of pub in NE end of village near end of Farley Lane. 6.4 miles. Pub, bus. SP394178.

The word Riding is from the Old English 'clearing', indicating that this was originally part of the ancient Wychwood Forest. Bear right at the junction with Boot Street (noting the Diamond Jubilee plaques for both Queen Victoria and Queen Elizabeth II) and continue down the hill to bear left at the next junction into the narrow Witney Lane towards Spratt's Farm. After passing two cottages on the left and just after the corrugated iron barn, turn left (SE) at the waymark on a footpath down a stony track. Enter the woods via a wooden gate and when the path divides after 40 yards, go left, descending through this beechwood. On meeting a track at the base of the wood, turn right to follow the eastern boundary of Stockey Plantation. Follow the track past the stables in the field in Stockey Bottom to go out of the wood turning left back to the bridge and the meeting place of paths just north of the River Evenlode.

The History of Stonesfield

This is a village built from the local limestone and roofed with the Stonesfield stone slates for which it is famous. It was here that the first fossil bones of a dinosaur (Megalosaurus) were found and described by William Buckland, an Oxford professor, in 1824. Buckland was an eminent scientist, but rather eccentric, for example, he decided to eat his way through the whole of the animal kingdom. At the end of this marathon he could not decide whether bluebottle or mole was the most unpleasant! The production of Stonesfield slates has a curious history. The stone was mined, put on the surface in clamps (heaps), and covered with soil in order to keep the slates moist. Then, in winter when frost was expected, the church bells were tolled and, regardless of the time of the day, the quarrymen were summoned to uncover the stones. After exposure to the frost, the blocks of stone could be split readily into thin roof tiles.

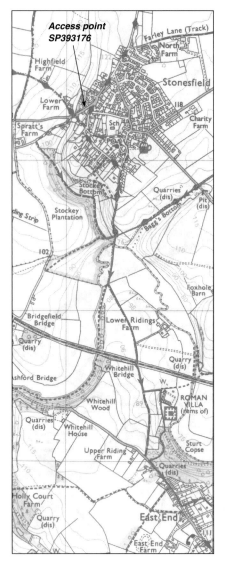

Back at the River Evenlode, cross the wooden bridge onto a bridleway across the field (S, 188°). Go through a small wooden gate beside a field gate to follow a track uphill (SE, 152°) ignoring a path that goes into the wood on the right. Go by a pair of double gates passing a track that goes left to Lower Ridings Farm. Keep ahead to follow the lane to go over the railway from Oxford to Moreton-in-Marsh. 200 yards after the railway bridge, turn left downhill on the footpath to the small cottage at the entrance of the North Leigh Roman Villa.

North Leigh Roman Villa

Roman mosaic, North Leigh

The occupants of this villa were likely to have been Romanised British farmers and perhaps people of some importance within the local native tribe of the Dobunni, selling their surplus food to the local townsfolk of Corinium (Cirencester) and Alchester (near Bicester). They lived here in the most prosperous period of the Roman occupation, and this site is of palatial proportions. There are tessellated pavements and hypocausts which are the Roman version of underfloor heating.

The site is managed by English Heritage and is open all the year. Access to the Roman mosaics is only possible on some summer weekends but they can be seen through the glass window of the low wooden building in the SW corner of the site.

After visiting the villa, turn sharp left (S) along the outside of the perimeter wall, to continue across the field (S, 175°) towards a wood. Go over a stile and, after a few yards, keep to the right and ascend through Sturt Copse, always keeping to the right at any fork.

Sturt Copse is an ancient wood-
land with several plant species
such as dog's mercury, wild
garlic, sanicle and spurge laurel,
which all indicate its antiquity.
We saw the uncommon blue
clustered bellflower here in July.

Clustered bellflower

Leave the wood to turn left (SE)
and go along the road into the
village of **East End**. Continue
walking past a footpath to the
right and a road called Sturt Wood
on the left. Then at a 30mph
repeater sign, and before a house
called 'Midway', turn left onto a
footpath between narrow hedges
to pass through a small paddock
and onto a lane. Turn right along
the lane to a small triangular
green. Here turn left past a house
called 'Evenlode Cottage' and down to turn right (E) along the field edge
toward the woods. Here there is a wet-weather option (*see below*).

At the edge of the wood, cross a stream by a small footbridge, and
after 20 yards turn right (S) onto the Wychwood Way and follow the path
near the edge of Abel Wood.

Wet weather option

When water levels are high, the walk beside the Evenlode can be
very wet. If you suspect you might get bogged down, then turn left
at the edge of the wood, following The Wychwood Way, descending
(NE) down to a footbridge along a well-marked track. Continue (NE)
over the open field to walk near the River Evenlode, then over
another footbridge crossing the river. Pass over the railway bridge
and climb up the steep slope of the river cliff, joining a lane (NE)
uphill towards the road. Here turn right (SE) and descend past the
Combe railway halt to the lane that leads right to the mill parking, or
left up to the Combe Lodge parking.

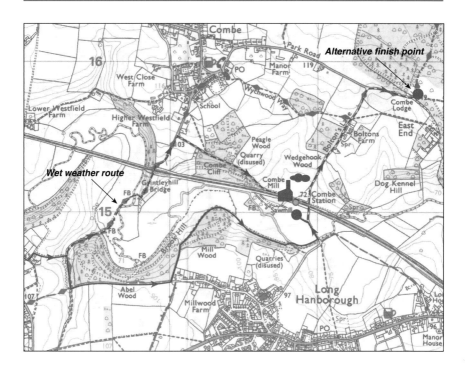

The area around here is farmed organically and there is a remarkable mixture of flowers. We saw the dark, purply-blue tufted vetch, the spherical clockheads of goatsbeard or 'Jack-go-to-bed-at-noon' (because the flower-heads close up at midday), pink and white striped bindweed and orchids thick on the banks.

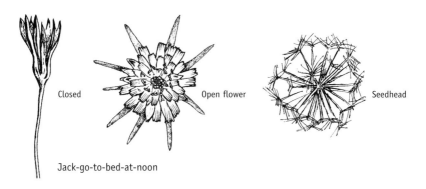

Closed   Open flower   Seedhead

Jack-go-to-bed-at-noon

Go through the gap in the trees and at the crossroads of paths, turn left (E) onto a restricted byway along the edge of the wood. When you reach houses on the very edge of Long Hanborough, turn left (N), still on the edge of Abel Wood. At the field edge, bear right (NE) on the footpath alongside Mill Wood showing that we are nearing Combe Mill. Continue on curving round (SE) between the wood and the River Evenlode to arrive at a big wooden gate and stile. Follow the footpath beside the wire fence to where a wooden-slatted footbridge turns right. Cross the bridge to turn left to follow the river path on its southern bank through a former quarry and out onto the road. Turn left over the river bridge taking care of the traffic, to turn left along the drive of Combe Mill.

Combe Mill

Combe Mill, on the river Evenlode, has existed since Saxon times and is mentioned in the Domesday Book of 1086 in connection with the village of 'Cube', which is known to have been Combe even though the present village was moved from the river valley in the 14th century, probably as the result of the Black Death.

Combe beam engine

In 1852 a beam (steam) engine was built to provide additional power to supplement that of the water wheel. The mill machinery including the forge blower enabled black-smith work and wood sawing to be done, as the increased reliability meant that the work could go on regardless of the flow of the river.

The mill, now run as a working industrial museum by the Combe Mill Society, is in steam on the third Sunday of each month (March–October) and open Wednesdays and Sundays (April–October). Toilets and tearoom.

For opening times and admission prices, Tel: 01993 358694 or www.combemill.org

East & West Hanney

Start and finish point SU414929

A walk in the floodplain of the River Ock, a tributary of the River Thames. The many place names ending in '-ey' from the Old English for 'island' reflect the fact that villages we pass through were once islands in marshy ground. The mills range from the ancient to the very modern, using water to power our homes rather than producing flour to power our bodies.

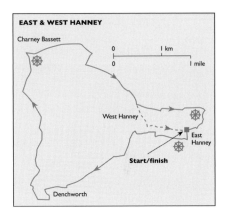

Distance: 8.4 miles (13.5 km).

Maps: Explorer 170 – Abingdon, Wantage & Vale of White Horse.
Landranger 174 – Newbury, Wantage & surrounding area.

Transport: Buses
• Stagecoach 31, X30. Oxford–East Hanney–Wantage.
• Stanford in the Vale Community Bus.
Wantage–Lyford–Denchworth–Charney Bassett.
Wed & Sat. Tel. 01367 710494.
www.stanford-in-the-vale.co.uk/pdf/bustimetable.pdf

Taxis: Grove
Wantage
• Evenlode Taxis. Tel: 01235 762035.
• Stuart's Taxis. Tel: 01235 770608.
• Supercab Taxis. Tel: 01235 770000.
• Webb's of Wantage. Tel: 01235 772000,
mob: 07881 647777.

Car Parking: Hanney War Memorial Hall car park SU414929 (OX12 0JL).

69

Accommodation/Public Houses/Refreshments:

East Hanney   • Black Horse PH. Tel: 01235 868212.
www.theblackhorseateasthanney.co.uk
• La Fontana Italian Restaurant, B&B. Tel: 01235 868287.
www.la-fontana.co.uk
• Hanney Community Shop. Tel: 01235 867408.

Denchworth   • The Fox Inn. Tel: 01235 868258.
www.thefoxdenchworth.co.uk

Charney   • The Chequers Inn. Tel: 01235 868642.
Bassett   www.chequerscharney.co.uk

West Hanney   • The Plough Inn. Tel: 01235 868674.
www.theploughwesthanney.co.uk

Wantage   • Accommodation see:
www.cotswolds.info/places/wantage

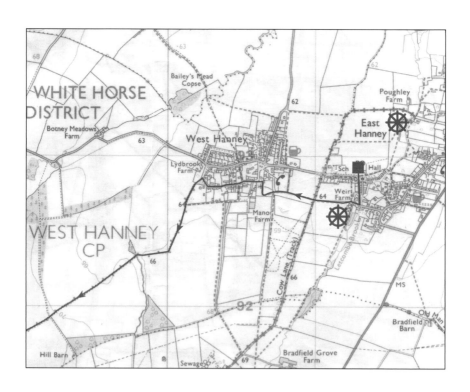

· From the Hanney Memorial Hall, turn right out of the car park entrance and immediately left (S) down the road called The Causeway, the name for a raised walkway above wet ground. Follow the road until we get our first glimpse of Letcombe Brook, a clear chalk stream originating in Letcombe Bassett (*see Wantage Mill walk, p.163*), on the left. Curve left to cross the Letcombe Brook over the bridge. On the right is the large red brick building of Dandridge's Mill with the Archimedes screw beyond it on the left (*see box below*). Beware of the traffic on this narrow road.

Dandridge's Mill, East Hanney

This water-driven mill was built in 1820 as a silk throwing mill, where raw silk fibres were cleaned, twisted together and wound onto bobbins. The work was done by Napoleonic War prisoners, but when the silk trade collapsed it became a grain mill. The mill continued operating until World War II when it was turned into an engineering works and used for making parts of the Mosquito Bomber aircraft.

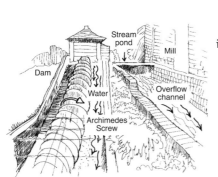

The building has now been converted into luxury apartments using the latest low-carbon technology, including the first domestic Archimedes power screw in the UK to produce electricity — this has reduced the carbon footprint of the building by 91%. It can be seen in action in the millrace beside the building. The force of the cascading water turns the central shaft of the screw which is linked to a generator.

There is an interpretation board about the Letcombe Brook on the lawn.

Retrace your steps over the bridge to Mill House, to take the footpath (W), marked 'West Hanney ½'. Cross the farmyard of Weir Farm, another reference to the watery surroundings, to follow on the left side of the hedgerow across the ancient green lane called Cow Lane (an indication of the former movement of cattle to and from their feeding meadows to the farm). Continue on the right side of the hedgerow, crossing to the left side of the hedge after the second kissing gate. On meeting a footpath going left, go through the third kissing gate and follow the path along the right side of **West Hanney** churchyard to the north church door. The origin of the name Hanney relates to *hanena ieg* (-ey) which means 'island frequented by wild cocks'.

St James the Great, West Hanney and the Hanney brooch

In the churchyard we noticed that many of the gravestones refer to people as from Berkshire; however, since the county boundary changes in 1974, West Hanney is now in Oxfordshire. The church stands on an ancient Saxon site which was probably a wooden construction as the first place of worship. Only the two stone coffins in the porch remain. The Normans then built the chevron-patterned porch on its twisted shafts and handsomely-carved capitals. Inside the church the tub-shaped font is carved with delicate vertical bands of rosettes.

The Hanney brooch, discovered in West Hanney in 2009, was buried with the corpse of a twenty-five-year-old woman. It is a rare 7th century Saxon brooch, with red garnets and gold inlay, and is on display at the Oxfordshire County Museum in Woodstock.

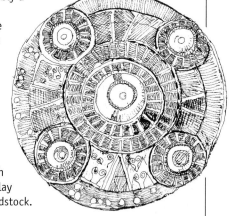

The Hanney brooch

An unusual cobbled path leads from the Norman church gate, its cobbles are end-on and it continues as a raised pavement beside the road beyond, another indication that this was a wet district. Across the road facing the church is the Old Vicarage, a fine red-brick chequered-diaperwork house with a Stonesfield slate roof and brick gate piers. To the left are the tall curved gables of the Georgian West Hanney House.

At the church gate turn left (W) along Church Street passing the 16th-century Plough Inn with its thatched roof. Continue along ignoring the first footpath on the left marked 'Grove 2'. We chose the village street route in order to see the mixture of ancient and modern houses. Deans Farm House to the left, Shepherd's Cottage on the right and Loader's Cottage on the left are reminders of the rural past. Curve right past the black-and-white timbered, thatched cottage on the left to a Restricted Byway (SW) marked 'Denchworth 1½'.

Restricted Byways

A Restricted Byway is different to an ordinary byway since it means that as well as pedestrians, cyclists and horseriders, it can be used by horse-drawn carriages and some classes of mobility vehicles for the disabled. They were previously known as RUPPs (Roads Used as Public Paths).

Follow this byway across the fields with good views ahead of the chalk escarpment of the Berkshire Downs and the Sparsholt Firs radio mast beside the Ridgeway. Go over a ditch where there are a few trees and keep the ditch on your left. The spotmark on the map measures 66m above sea level — not very high! Ahead is the mainline railway between London and Bristol.

When we walked through in August, the fields were a pale gold with the ripening wheat and the ditches had red admiral and peacock butterflies feeding on the ragwort and sow thistle flowers.

At a crossroads in the track, where to the left are the ruins of Hill Barn, go ahead and keep on the track towards the buildings of **Denchworth**. On reaching the road, turn left (SE), taking care to walk on the outside verges for safety's sake, for 230 yards. We chose this route rather than turning right towards the village, since it is a narrow, dangerous road into the village. At a footpath sign 'Denchworth ½' turn right (W) through a narrow wood, then across a field (W) to cross a footbridge over the Childrey Brook. Continue on the path (NW) to arrive in the Denchworth churchyard, where there is an ancient preaching cross.

On leaving the churchyard (N), there is the base of another ancient preaching cross on the small green outside, and just past Fox Cottage on the wall is a dark wooden niche with a Roll of Honour inside. The long, massive building of the Fox Inn was originally a pub with barns and by walking a few yards along the road to the left, it is possible to see the huge thatched roof through the gateway of the pub.

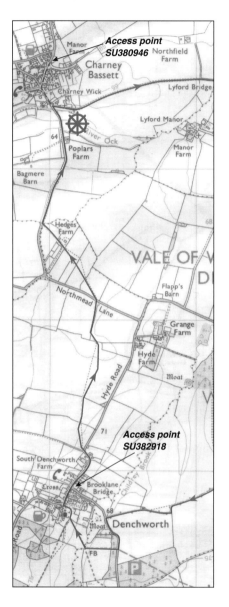

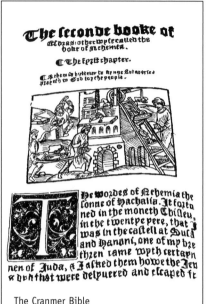

The Cranmer Bible

Denchworth Church

Denchworth church has a Norman doorway and inside, a copy of the Cranmer Bible under a tapestry cover. It has monumental brasses to the Hyde family, whose name is reflected in some of the local place names, and the distinctive pinks, crimsons and greens in the stained-glass windows by Burne-Jones. The organ was played by Mary Hardy, who was sister of the author Thomas Hardy and the village school mistress.

On the right is the wide gated entrance of Denchworth Manor with its two small gatehouse cottages on either side of it. The medieval moated manor house itself is not visible from the road.

Access point: Denchworth 3 miles, pub, bus. SU382918.

From the Fox Inn take the road marked 'Charney Bassett 2' (N) to walk through the village on Hyde Road passing the former school house on the left where Mary Hardy taught, now a private house. Pass the Old Post Office on the right with its steeply pitched roof indicating that it had previously been thatched, and past College Farm on the left. Continue walking out of the village (NNW) for 50 yards, taking care of the traffic, to bear left over a stile across three fields (NNE, 20°). There are good views of the Faringdon Folly Hill to the left with its clump of fir trees, and Hyde Farm to the right. At the second stile, bear further right, then diagonally left at the hedge to another two stiles in the hedge-rows. At the third stile and footbridge, turn sharp left, across the corner of the field, to go over another stile and turn right alongside the hedgerow to reach Northmead Lane. Cross the road with care, to enter Northmead Farm land, and immediately turn left over a wooden stile by a metal gate and across the field. Do not go along the cinder track straight ahead. Bear diagonally left (NW) to a stile two thirds of the way along the hedge (NW, 340°) and into the horse paddocks, then over the stile by the left-hand oak tree. Continue in the same direction to a stile through the hedge left of the main farm gates of Hedges Farm. Go left of a pond with bulrushes, cross the farm drive, over another stile and across another paddock (NW) to a footpath leading directly onto the road via a footbridge. Turn right (N) and, taking care of the traffic, walk for nearly a mile, past Poplars Farm. Cross the main channel of the River Ock, then the arched stone bridge over the original river course. The flow was diverted to prevent flooding the village of **Charney Bassett**.

Access point: Charney Bassett, pub, 4.8 miles. SU380946.

Charney Bassett
The name of the village means 'island on the Charn' (an old name for the River Ock), and Bassett refers to Ralph Bassett, a 12th-century landowner and the Justiciar or chief minister of England. Although the mill is along the road to the right, it is worth continuing (NW) along Main Street passing Charney Wick to the right (Old English *wic* = dairy farm) to reach the village green with its remains of an ancient market cross, war memorial and pub.

Cat masks

To continue our route retrace your steps back to the stone bridge over the Ock, then along the road marked Lyford, passing the village church to the left.

It is worth admiring the intricately stone-carved Norman doorways on both the north and the south sides. The south doorway arch is decorated with cat masks. These feline faces have long leaves flowing from their mouths. This was a traditional style of architecture later associated with the depiction of the Green Man (see Ascott walk, p.13 and Pitstone walk, p.117).

Charney Mill is a small, easily-overlooked, elm-boarded building on the right beyond Mill Cottage, and the entrance to Charney Manor, which is a Quaker retreat, is to the left.

From the mill, continue (E) towards **Lyford** (meaning 'ford where flax grew') for just under 1 mile crossing the River Ock at Lyford Bridge. This lane is a quiet, narrow route, but traffic can be fast, so take care.

This is the floodplain of the River Ock and in March we enjoyed the huge cloud formations visible over this flat landscape. At Lyford Bridge we noticed that the river flows north towards the River Thames.

Charney Mill (SU382944)

Charney was one of 31 manors held by Abingdon Abbey early in the 12th century. Charney Manor was originally the residence of the Abbey's bailiff or steward. These Benedictine monks were renowned for their water-engineering skills, and created the mill stream by taking water from the River Ock. The source of water for the mill was diverted in 1974 to prevent persistent flooding in the village. The buildings date from 1807, using elm as the main structure, with oak for the waterwheel shaft. The undershot waterwheel, which is the wheel driven by the flow of the steam passing under it, was taken to Abingdon Abbey Mill and worked throughout World War II. The original millstones are in the former Upper Reaches Hotel (built on the site of the Abbey) and the present metal wheel in Charney is from St Helen's Mill in Abingdon! The arrangement of the building is typical for a corn mill of its period with a bin floor, stone floor and ground floor.

Open on National Mills Weekend or contact Bruce Hedge, Tel: 01235 210612, email: bruce.hedge@ntlworld.com.
For groups, contact P. Coldwell, Tel: 01235 868677.

After the bridge ignore the footpath sign to the left before Brook Cottages, but take the footpath to the right just past Brook Cottages. (NB If there are cattle in the field, we advise continuing on to turn right into a small lane towards Lyford to pass the 18th-century Alms Court on the right.) If the field is empty go over the metal gate to bear left (S) to the stile in the far side of the field and left along the enclosed footpath. On meeting the road turn right then left past the drive to the Old Vicarage. (NB the footpath (W–E) marked on the map no longer exists). One hundred and fifty yards further on, at the sharp turn right, leave

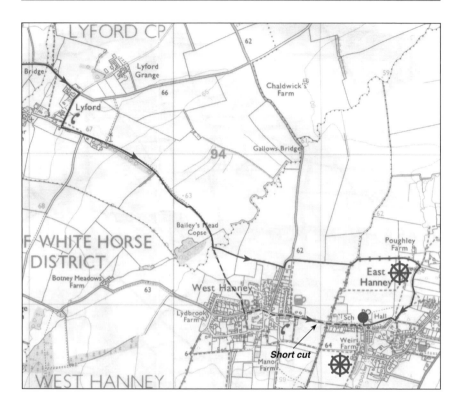

the road to take a footpath on a concreted drive marked 'West Hanney 1'. Go along the left side of a corrugated iron barn, then in the same direction (SE) follow the track along the left side of a tall hedge. Keep on the left side of the long linear wood and cross a small field (S, 180°) with Bailey's Mead Copse to the right. Cross over the Childrey Brook via a foot-bridge. Here is an option to take a short cut (*see box on facing page*) back to West Hanney Village Hall, but which misses out Lower Mill and the walk beside Letcombe Brook.

To opt for the longer route, take the left-hand of the two paths (E) to cross a field, then on in the same direction in the second field to walk along the left side of a hedgerow that leads to a footbridge onto Water Lane. Turn left (N) along the road for 100 yards, then right (E) across the fields through a wooden kissing gate to meet a byway. Turn left along a twisting green lane (E), passing Poughley Farm to the left to arrive at a T-junction of tracks. Turn right to reach the bridge over the Letcombe Brook below the millrace of Lower Mill.

Short Cut

Alternative short-cut route from Bailey's Mead Copse to West Hanney village (saves 0.3 miles). From the footbridge over Childrey Brook, take the right-hand of the two paths towards the buildings of the village and across two fields to arrive back in the village. Turn left (E) along Main Street to pass the triangular green and continue along the footpath of School Road leaving it at the sharp right-hand bend to arrive back at the Village Hall.

Lower Mill, East Hanney

Chequer pattern with vitrified headers

Walling on north front

Rubbed brick

Blue brick

Lower Mill is a tall brick building with a sack hoist. It was built in 1812 by the West family, who also owned Venn Mill. The mill was burnt out in 1903 and is now a private house even though the water wheel inside the building remains. We noticed that house martins have nested under the sack hoist.

Facing the mill upstream, go through the green-painted metal kissing gate on the left side of the mill, to follow the course of Letcombe Brook. There are old orchards on the left and interpretation boards along the way. Ignore any paths leading away from the brook, but keep beside the water where there are the remains of stepping stones.

At an iron bridge, the board explains that the barrier was erected in the 19th century to prevent cows coming into the village. It originally had a turnstile at both ends. The fast-flowing, clear waters provide a habitat for the bullhead, a fish also known as Miller's Thumb, which hides under the stones and feeds on shrimps and insects.

Turn right over the iron bridge and immediately left, still near the river bank behind the houses, to turn right along a path between houses to turn left into Brookside and along to the Memorial Hall and car park.

Venn Mill, Garford, near Wantage (SU429949)

Venn Mill also gains its power from the River Ock. It is sited 1 mile north-east of East Hanney, on the busy Oxford/Wantage road (A338), but has no easy footpath access. It is well worth a visit when it is working on National Mills weekends.

There has been a mill on this site beside the Childrey Brook since it was recorded in Domesday Book in 1086. On the 1761 map it was called 'Ben's Mill'. The present buildings date from about 1800 and were advertised in the *Reading Mercury* as 'all new built Water Corn Mill', complete with the Mill House, now with the road dividing the buildings. It is a three-storey building with superb carpentry in the bin floor, with its roof timbers, central walkway and grain bins. A small waterwheel would pull a cable that went across the road into the miller's house ringing an alarm bell in times of flood. The two millstones consist of French Burrs, that is, they are made up of segments of rock called chert, a variety of quartz quarried in an area near Paris.

National Mills Weekend opening, or by appointment, contact Ian Smith, Tel: 01367 240405, email: ianlinsmith@hotmail.com

Great Haseley

Start and finish point SP644016

A walk first across the low-lying floodplain of the River Thame, then visiting the remains of the noble parkland in Ascott Park. The route goes through the picturesque villages of Great Haseley, Little Milton, Stadhampton (with its watermill) and Great Milton. We cross the land of Wells Farm, with its rich biodiversity created by traditional management. Above this land is the domain of the red kites. The walk concludes by passing the recently restored windmill above Great Haseley.

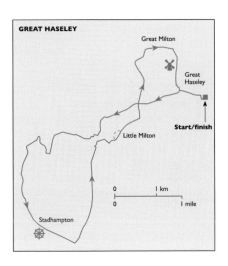

Distance: 10.5 miles (16.9 km).

Maps: Explorer 180 – Oxford, Witney & Woodstock.
Explorer 170 – Abingdon, Wantage & Vale of White Horse.
Landranger 164 – Oxford.

Transport: Buses
- Great Haseley 103.
- Great Milton 103, 104. Heyfordian. Tel: 01869 241500.
- Stadhampton T1. Thames Travel. Tel: 01491 837988.

Taxis: Milton Common
Wheatley
Stadhampton
Oxford
- Cab Co Britannia. Tel: 01844 279100.
- Cozier Executive Travel. Tel: 01865 436120.
- Courtesy Cars. Tel: 01865 343575.
- ABC Radio Taxis. Tel: 01865 242424.

Car Parking: Wide drive near St Peter's church, Great Haseley, on the east side of the village. SP644016 (OX44 7JY).

Accommodation/Public Houses/Refreshments:

Little Milton	• The Village Shop (serves snacks and coffee). Tel: 01844 279978.
	• The Lamb PH. Tel: 01844 279527. www.littlemilton.org.uk
Stadhampton	• The Crown Inn. Tel: 01865 890381.
Great Milton	• The Bull. Tel: 01844 279726.
Great Haseley	• The Plough Inn. Tel: 01844 279283. www.ploughpub.com
Chiselhampton	• The Coach and Horses, B&B (0.7 miles from Stadhampton). Tel: 01865 890255. www.coachhorsesinn.co.uk

---

A land of 'gentle families'

In the 16th and 17th centuries a large number of 'gentle', well-established families were attracted to this area because the villages were situated on small rises above the flood plain, the water was good and there was excellent, easily-quarried stone for building. It was obviously an innovative area since there are records that James Wells of Little Milton tried to introduce threshing machines in 1830, but there were riots, and the villagers from Drayton, Chiselhampton and Stadhampton broke his machinery. Six rioters were arrested and sentenced to seven years' transportation, the likely destination being Australia. Today, peace has returned, and the carefully renovated manor houses and thatched cottages attract commuters from London.

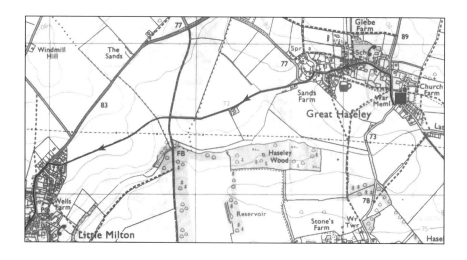

From the church, walk along the formal drive (W) in front of the Manor House, through the high gate pillars with two oval oculi (holes, from the Latin for 'eye') in the left-hand pillar, to then turn right (N) joining the main village street (W) towards Great Milton. Many of the cottages are built of rubble, some timber-framed with steeply pitched thatched roofs.

Great Haseley Manor House oculi

Pass the Plough Inn on the left and Horse Close Cottages. At the western end of the village join a tarmac bridleway past Sands Farm on the left. The first glimpse of the windmill can be seen by looking back to the hill to the right (N). There are fine views to the Chiltern Hills scarp edge to the left (S). The M40 cutting through the scarp, and the Stokenchurch mast are visible. Continue along the bridleway to cross a footbridge which is the boundary of the Wells Farm land.

Wells Farm Nature Reserve
This 163 acre farm demonstrates that modern farming practices and environmental conservation can work in harmony. There are six-metre-wide field margins that have been sown with wild flower seed mix. These margins then produce a habitat for butterflies and a winter food source for mixed flocks of finches, skylarks, yellowhammers and the increasingly rare corn buntings.

Corn bunting

Running from north to south is a wide grassy bank crossing the arable fields. This is a beetle bank providing cover for spiders and beetles such as ladybirds which act as pest control for the neighbouring fields. In some of the fields are skylark plots. These are plots, often described as the size of a typical living room, which are left unseeded (the farmer lifts his seeding drill for a few moments) thus providing an area of short grass on which the ground-nesting skylarks can breed and their chicks can thrive in. These initiatives throughout the country have dramatically increased skylark numbers. We saw a fox, hares and roe deer.

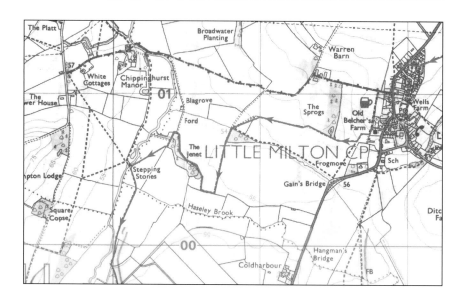

Go past a crossing bridleway to walk beside the alder trees and a laid hedge. Wild privet, with its small black berries in winter, grows here. The square church tower of **Little Milton** village is ahead and to the left. Enter the village via Old Field cul-de-sac. Go along this road to meet the main Thame Road. (NB The Village Shop, selling snacks and flour from the Wessex Mill in Wantage, is 30 yards to the right). Turn left (SE) beside the village street taking great care of the busy traffic, passing Boundary House on the right, Reformation Cottage on the left and ignoring the byway which leaves the High Street just after Crofter's Close. Instead, continue past the ancient Lamb Inn with its cruck beams, down the High Street, branching right at the junction signposted Stadhampton and down to the church.

It is worth noticing the two romantic 'cottages ornés' on the left 20 yards beyond the church lych gate. These cottages formed the lodge gate to Milton House beyond.

Cottages ornés

An enclosed footpath leads from just before the church (W). At the end, turn left then right onto a footpath beside a field. Follow the hedgerow on the right (SW) for only 50 yards before branching right (W) towards the southern end of the woodland, called The Sprogs, with its pond. Continue along this path (W) to reach a hedgerow. Cross the footbridge over a ditch and go diagonally left through the young wood to then turn left (S) over a concrete bridge and along the right side of another wood, then across a field. At the field end, before a ditch, the path turns right and right again to go alongside the east side of the wood called The Jenet. At the corner of the wood, turn left (SW). Go along part of the west side of the wood, then at the open metal gates, bear right (SW, 242°) across the flood meadow towards some tall willow trees and to the river edge where there are stepping stones (*see OS map*).

Only when the water level of the River Thame is low is this a possible crossing place, so it is not part of the route. However, as the map shows, it was an ancient crossing since several footpaths converge at this point; there are plans to reinstate it.

Instead, from this spot, facing away from the river, bear half right (SE, 168°) to a stile near the east corner of the field and a footbridge over the Haseley Brook. In the next field, follow the path along the right side of the wire fence (SW) to pass close to the river.

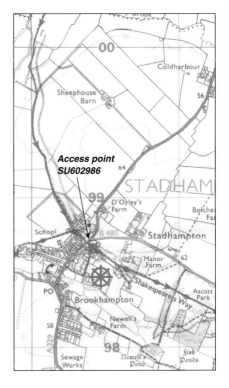

These are quiet meadows and we saw roe deer, a heron, buzzards and heard skylarks.

Keep near to the hedge and go through a gap into the next field, then 50 yards further on, at a metal gate with a waymark, bear left through the gate and cross the small field skirting round the corner of fir trees concealing a pond. Cross the stile in the SE corner to turn right (S) into a green lane which forms Copson Lane and follow this for 0.7 miles into the village of **Stadhampton**. On arriving at the village green it is worth visiting the church to the left which has some impressive brasses. To reach it go in front of a brick farmhouse with a railing fence and pass the Old Vicarage. If not visiting the church, turn right towards the pub and village shop.

Access Point: Stadhampton, 4.8 miles. Pub, bus, shop, PO, B&B (0.7 miles from route). SU602986.

From the pub, turn left (NE) to take the footpath (SE) waymarked 'Chalgrove 3' alongside the south edge of the large village green. Thirty yards from the waymark, there is a lane and footpath on the right, just after a house called 'Greenway'. This is the entrance to Stadhampton watermill.

Stadhampton Watermill
(SU604985)

This is a three-storey brick-built watermill which last worked in 1945. The large millpond is now dry, but its overshot wheel and machinery are turned using water electrically pumped from the brook. An overshot wheel is the most efficient since it has the double advantage of both the weight and the momentum of the falling water striking the paddles.

Open on National Mills Weekends, 2–6, or contact Mrs J. R. Peet, Tel: 01865 890378.

Ascott Park

A large meadow surrounds the site of the former manor house of the Dormer family, one of the 'gentle families' (see *Quainton walk, p.129*). The original house was attacked by John Hampden in the Civil War (see *Lacey Green walk, p.93*). Then sadly the rebuilt house, described as 'a verie noble house', burned to the ground in 1662 when wood shavings caught fire just as construction was finishing. There are several interpretation boards explaining the history. Only the dovecote, a garden pavilion, the fishponds, and the tall gate piers at the end of one of the 300-year-old lime avenues survive. The dovecote, in particular, is an attractive structure, built in a rich orange brick with a Flemish bond and lime mortar.

Dovecotes were used to provide birds and eggs for the table and to provide manure for the garden. In the 16th and 17th centuries pigeon dung provided a major source of saltpetre for the making of gunpowder. However, the Parliamentarians in the Civil War blew up dovecotes because they believed pigeons fed off the land of the ordinary people and only the landlord got the benefit!

(*Source: Oxfordshire Buildings Trust and Oxfordshire County Council*).

Ascott Park dovecote

Continue along the edge of the village green, past the play area to approach the right side of the Manor House. Before Cat Lane, turn left through a small gate onto a footpath beside a tall wooden fence towards Ascott Park. This path is also part of the Shakespeare's Way, a long-distance footpath from Stratford on Avon to the Globe Theatre in London. On arriving at some trees, cross the right of two stiles to enter Ascott Park. Follow the path to bear slightly right, away from the avenue of lime trees to enjoy this peaceful parkland.

If you decide not to follow the trail, go across the park on the footpath (SE) to rejoin the Shakespeare's Way. Go over a stile (E) towards the farm outbuildings south of **Ascott**, and through a metal gate to turn left (N) along the farm track. Instead of taking a footpath (the Shakespeare's Way) that goes to the right (E), continue towards the B480 road (N) past Piccadilly Cottages.

The cottages are so-called because this road junction was known as Piccadilly Corner. A local farmer told us that during World War II both nearby farms housed a number of evacuees and this was a busy community. People still ask to alight at Piccadilly Corner at the Thames Travel bus stop.

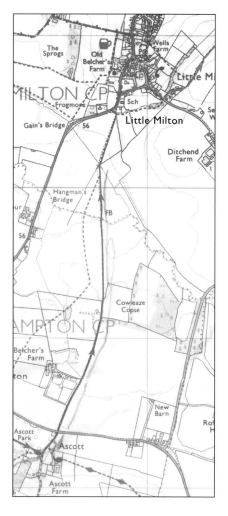

Cross the road with care to follow a tarmac track (N) marked 'Little Milton 1¾' past Belcher's Farm and a locked green metal gate to a large field gate at the end of the track. Bear away from the wire fence on the right. Cross a large field half left (N, 358°), aiming for the electricity pylon on the horizon which is the first one left (W) of Little Milton church tower. Another nearer landmark is the whitened trunk of a tree struck by lightning. On reaching the right-hand stile in a wire fence, cross a narrow strip of grass ahead to go over a footbridge in the next hedgerow. (*A helpful hint: this bridge can be confused with a wide metal gate leading to a bridge for farm vehicles further to the right (E). If this does happen turn left on the far side of the bridge and go (NW) along the hedge for about 150 yards to the small footbridge.*) From the footbridge bear left (N) across another field to go over a footbridge and ditch in the hedgerow at SP001617. Then bear diagonally right (NE, 20°) across the next field, aiming directly for the tower of Little Milton church, to then veer right to a stile at the end of a garden hedge on the south side of **Little Milton** village. A dark house with three white dormer windows is a good landmark. Although there is a footpath going right (E) behind the village, we have chosen to go along the road to enjoy the traditional architecture.

So, at the waymark, go over the stile along a narrow path between allotments and houses to turn right onto the main village street. Pass the village school on the right, then turn right into Gold Street passing thatched buildings and the large manor house on the left. Bear right at a small triangular green at the southern end of Little Milton and turn right past 'Four Trees'.

Sweet violets

When we passed in February the left hand garden bank was covered in sweet-smelling violets. We lay on our tummies to smell them!

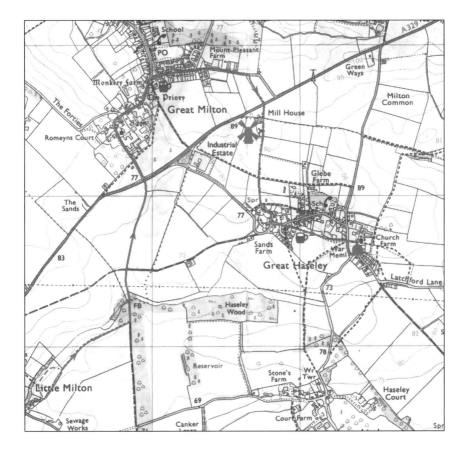

Go down the lane to turn left at the waymark to 'Great Haseley 1' before Linnet Cottage along the track up beside Blenheim Cottages. At a metal gate, turn right up some steps to turn left (NE) along the right side of a hedge. We are back in Wells Farm Nature Reserve. At the metal gate mentioned above there is an option to go through the gate to follow the valley below through a wildflower walk beside the stream where a barn owl regularly hunts. This path joins the upper path at the end of the meadow. At the end of the path turn left onto the bridleway (N) with a wire fence and wood to the right. Cross the footbridge to meet a crossing bridleway in the open field (*NB this could be an option for turning right for a short cut back to Great Haseley*). Continue north beside another wire fence, with good views of the windmill to the right. Cross the busy A329 road and walk along the road towards **Great Milton** village. Follow the village street to enjoy a rich mixture of traditional architecture.

Great Milton Village

The manor house south of the church was originally 15th-century, and is now occupied by the world-famous Belmond Le Manoir aux Quat'Saisons hotel and restaurant. It has a beautiful 17th-century gateway just north of the restaurant entrances. The great house opposite the church is dated 1720. St Mary's Church has a remarkable monument containing the three effigies of the Dormer family (see Ascott Park). Monkery Farm (The Monkery) on the left is dated as 15th century. Further along the street, the Priory on the right has a 16th century façade with mullioned windows. The triangular green is surrounded by some terraces of 17th and 18th century thatched cottages, the Bull pub being of the same age.

If the church is not open, the key can be obtained from the reception desk at Le Manoir restaurant. Rector, Tel: 01844 279498.

Turn right at the triangular green (E) by the pub, to walk along the Thame road passing Mount Pleasant Farm. Where the row of houses on the left ends, turn right into Old Field onto a footpath (SE) that follows the left side of a hedgerow to cross back over the A329. Although there is a notice indicating that the drive ahead is a private road, there is a waymark on the north side of the A329, so follow the footpath (S) past Mill House. Go over the footbridge left of a high hedge to arrive at the windmill beside the path.

Great Haseley Windmill (SP638024)

This is a stone-built tower mill built of Corallian limestone brought from the nearby Great Milton quarries. The history is somewhat uncertain, but it is thought that the mill was constructed in 1760 with common sails (meaning an open wooden frame which bears the sail cloth). Over time, the building fell into disrepair, but in 2005 a restoration trust was set up and both the exterior and the internal mill machinery have been restored. The ogee-shaped cap was replaced in 2013 and the sails in 2014.

It is possible to climb up from the stone floor to the bin floor and up to the cap floor. Here, the view is over an uninterrupted vista which makes the mill's position ideal for catching the prevailing wind.

Opening times only on National Mills Weekend while restoration is in progress.
www.greathaseleywindmill.net

Continue south on the footpath ignoring the crossing path to dogleg left and immediately right into a narrow path that joins Mill Lane and descends into **Great Haseley**.

This is an enchanting way, reminiscent of times past. The lane is unmetalled, all the cottages are thatched, and most are in the traditional position of end-on to the street.

On meeting the main village road, turn left (E) and, if you are not visiting the pub, then turn almost immediately right down the left-hand footpath from Horse Close. Go between houses to cross the remains of an old Cotswold stone stile on a footpath behind the houses towards the church. The back of the Old Rectory has a 'ha-ha' (a low stone wall instead of a fence to ensure an uninterrupted view across the countryside). Cross the road back to the church.

Lacey Green

Start and finish point SP823036

This walk starts from the high chalky scarp edge of the Chiltern Hills at Whiteleaf Cross. The route goes through beech woods and then south to Hampden House, a Strawberry Hill Gothic building, with Civil War connections. From there we climb the gentle slope to arrive at Lacey Green windmill, the oldest smock mill in England. At nearby Parslow's Hillock we discovered a snug bar once frequented by the war poet Rupert Brooke. We return to Whiteleaf Cross via beech 'hangers' carpeted with bluebells in springtime.

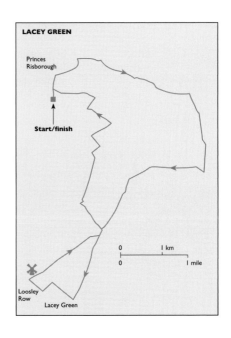

Distance: 8.4 miles (13.5 km).

Maps: Explorer 181 – Chiltern Hills North.
Landranger 165 – Aylesbury & Leighton Buzzard area.

Transport: Buses   • Arriva 120,121. Thame–Princes Risborough.
• Arriva 300. Aylesbury–Princes Risborough–Loosley Row–High Wycombe.
Rail   • Princes Risborough Station, Chiltern Line.

Taxis: Princes   • Fastline Taxis. Tel: 01844 275000.
Risborough   • Village Cars. Tel: 01844 342551.

Car Parking: Whiteleaf Hill car park and picnic site. From Monks Risborough go south-east along Peters Lane (signposted Whiteleaf). Car park is on the left (E), SP823036 (HP27 0RP).

Accommodation/Public Houses/Refreshments:

Lower Cadsden • The Plough PH and B&B (200 yards from route). Tel: 01844 343302. www.plough-at-cadsden.co.uk

Lacey Green • The Whip Inn. Tel: 01844 344060.

Loosely Row • Greenhills Garden Apartment B&B. Tel: 01844 342409. www.princesrisborough-bedbreakfast.co.uk

Parslow's Hillock • The Pink and Lily PH. Tel: 01494 489857. www.pinkandlily.co.uk

Princes Risborough • Information Centre, Tower Court, Horns Lane, HP27 0AJ. Tel: 01844 274795. e-mail: risborough_office@wycombe.gov.uk

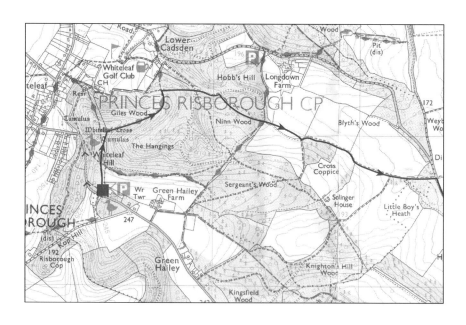

Leave the car park by passing the notice board and follow the path (NW) into the trees. On joining the larger track (a bridleway), turn right (N). This track is the Ridgeway, an ancient route stretching from Avebury in Wiltshire to Ivinghoe Beacon in Buckinghamshire.

Once in the woodland it is worth looking to the right where the World War I practice trenches described on the car park noticeboard can be seen. They are protected by their cover of dense vegetation. The trees are a mixture of native species such as hazel and beech.

Go through the gate to emerge on to the open downland.

Whiteleaf Hill Barrow

Immediately left are the remains of a Neolithic barrow, first excavated in the 1930s, with further finds made in the 1990s. It is one of the oldest monuments in Buckinghamshire. A man was buried here within a wooden mortuary house over 5,500 years ago and covered by a mound of soil or barrow. The noticeboard also describes how this rare piece of open chalk grassland gives the chalkhill blue and marbled white butterflies a rich source of nectar on which to feed. This hill is part of the scarp edge of the Chiltern Hills and from here there is a good view of the town of Princes Risborough below. On a clear day, looking SW, Wittenham Clumps can be seen in the middle distance, and on a very clear day the White Horse Hill on the Berkshire Downs (SW) is visible. Looking NE, we could see Coombe Hill near Wendover and Ivinghoe Beacon (NE) at the end of the scarp.

Whiteleaf Cross

Beyond the barrow, the huge Whiteleaf Cross, cut into the chalk, reaches the top of the scarp slope, though from this vantage point not much of the cross is visible. The first record of the cross was in 1742, and the reason for its creation is still unknown. Two hundred yards beyond the barrow (N) is a distinctive circular mound. This is probably a mill mound, the site of an old windmill which would have benefited from this windy spot.

At the waymark post just beyond the barrow, turn right to follow the Ridgeway into Giles Wood and down a steep slope for 700 yards.

In the shady spots beside the path, we saw white helleborine in June.

At a prominent waymark post where paths cross (SP826043), leave the Ridgeway and turn right (E).

After 70 yards at a waymark, where the route divides, take the narrow left-hand path, going first along the contours of the slope, then steeply downhill to meet several paths. In the base of the valley, aim for the waymark post with the purple sign beyond the triangular patch of green. Take this Purple Route (E, 100°) which is the left of the two major tracks on the right. Keep left at the next fork (by a fallen tree) to follow the valley bottom along an ancient sunken way between Hobb's Hill (N) and Ninn Wood (S).

This sunken way was known as Kings Street in Anglo-Saxon times, then Killington Way in medieval times. This is a shady area and in winter we noticed the thick moss on the fallen trunks. In summer, woodspurge was growing with spurge laurel, an indicator of an ancient wood.

Ascend the steeply-sided sunken way to reach a small stile beside a prominent ancient woodland bank. Cross the stile and dogleg left and right (SE, 124°) between more woodland banks, still on the Purple Route and into open fields. Keep on the left side of the hedge and then through a gap in the hedgerow, just left of a wood, at the end of the first field. Follow the left (N) side of Cross Coppice and continue (SE), descending gently down the dip slope of the escarpment to join an asphalt track in front of a coniferous wood. Turn left (E) along this track, to walk towards the road. At the road, turn right past the entrance to Hampden Chase (or Dirtywood Farm as it is marked on the map), to go south along the left-hand side of the road with its wide verges for 400 yards. Take care of the fast traffic.

Bowdlerisation of Place Names
The dictionary definition is "to expurgate, or purify of unpleasant matters". In the 19th century Thomas Bowdler and his wife edited Shakespeare, removing anything that might be found offensive, producing *The Family Shakespeare*, a text that could be read to women and children. At the road is the drive entrance of Hampden Chase, the new name of Dirtywood Farm (i.e. 'Muddy Wood Farm'), a modern example of bowdlerisation. Other examples are the numerous Grape Lanes which were originally Grope Lanes.

At the end of the wood, turn right at the waymark to follow the Chiltern Way (S) climbing gently across the field into beech and coniferous woods. Continue south up the wooded slope and out of the woods to continue in the same direction across a field towards the buildings of Hampden House.

Brimstone butterfly

In mid-March there were sulphur yellow Brimstone butterflies and a greater spotted woodpecker drumming to attract a mate.

On arriving at the back of Hampden House, walk beside the ha-ha on the left. The crenellations on the buildings to the left are part of Hampden House's distinctive Strawberry Hill Gothic architecture (so named since it was at Strawberry Hill in Twickenham, London, where Horace Walpole, a great setter of architectural style, built his 'little Gothic castle' in 1749.)

If not taking this diversion to the house, turn right at the gate.

From the gate walk (NW) along an avenue of oak trees. On reaching the open fields, instead of continuing (NW) on the main track (Grim's Ditch), bear left (W, 278°) beside a white post and head towards another small white post across a field on a minor footpath, in the direction of a circular coppice of trees (this is typical parkland to which the name of nearby Park Farm refers). On the far side of the coppice, go past two more white posts, then at the edge of the wood, at the third post, turn

John Hampden and Hampden House

John Hampden, cousin of Oliver Cromwell and a Member of Parliament, was prominent in opposing Charles I's attempts to impose a tax known as 'Ship Money' throughout the country rather than only on the ports that had traditionally paid it. This movement was one of the original causes of the Civil War. Hampden was killed at the Battle of Chalgrove as the Parliamentarian forces advanced towards Oxford in 1643. It is thought that Cromwell would have been less powerful had Hampden survived.

The core of the present house is Elizabethan and some of the ancient small brickwork can still be seen. By turning left after the gateway onto the drive it is possible to see some of the features of the Strawberry Hill Gothic such as the ogee-topped windows and the heraldic statues on top of the roof.

To see more detail of the architectural restoration of the interior of the house, there is a virtual tour at: www.hampdenweddings.com

Strawberry Hill House, London

right for 50 yards alongside its perimeter, then left at the fourth white post into the wood. Once in Barne's Grove, part of the beech woodland of the Hampden Estate, do not take the main track to the right along the edge of the wood, but follow a minor footpath (SW, 243°) marked with two white arrows along the Chiltern Way. Where a track joins from the right, bear left (SW) past a waymarker.

We noticed candlesnuff fungi (Xylaria hypoxylon). It is black at the base, grey in the middle and white at the tips, just like a snuffed candle wick.

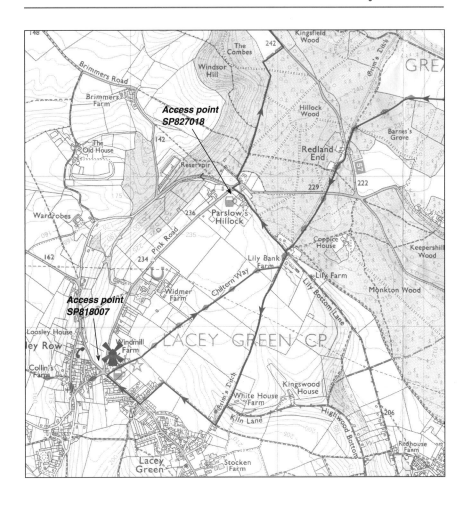

Candlesnuff fungi

> **Grim's Ditch**
> This substantial ditch is a pre-Roman Iron Age ditch and
> embankment. The name originates from the Saxons since they
> thought that anything unusual was the work of their pagan
> god, Grim, or Woden as he was called. Many embankments or
> ditches of this type are also be known as Devil's ditches. Most
> just delineated boundaries, though some were fortifications.

After about 50 yards beyond the waymarker post, the path meets the
NE/SW route of Grim's Ditch.

At Grim's Ditch, bear right to descend into the ditch, then climb up
left onto the rampart on the other side, to turn left (SW) along its route
to meet the road at Redland End. At the road go through a wooden
kissing gate, to dogleg left and right onto a minor road marked 'Lacey
Green 2'. This small hamlet is typical of a dispersed woodland settlement with flint-built cottages with brick used only as nogging at the
edges.

Follow the minor road to Lacey Green and here we are still following
the route of Grim's Ditch with trees on its banks to the right. The coppiced hazel trees indicate that the wood is ancient. Cross a road, go over
a stile, and onto a bridleway. Continue (SW) under an electricity pylon
along the footpath (The Chiltern Way) to descend towards Lily Bank
Farm. At the small road, dogleg left and right to follow the bridleway
(SW) along the right side of the farm. This is the beginning of an ancient
green lane which can be very muddy in wet weather. If you suspect this
is so, then you may prefer to take the route detailed in Option B.

Option A for dry weather
From the farm's brick wall follow the bridleway (SW) along the
line of Grim's Ditch gently uphill and then down into a small valley
past White House Farm to a junction of tracks. Turn right (NW) up
the slope and left to meet the road on the edge of Lacey Green
village. Turn right, past the bus stop to reach the track that leads to
the windmill and on towards the The Whip Inn.

Option B for wet weather

After only 100 yards, bear right at a waymark and go through a metal kissing gate on The Chiltern Way (SW), cross the field diagonally and another gate to cross another field diagonally right, keeping right of the electricity pylon. Cross a stile beside a metal gate in the far corner. Here there is a good view of Lacey Green windmill. As was the custom it is sited on the scarp edge to maximize the wind power. After the metal gate, continue SW along a fenced track through horse paddocks. Go down the cinder track, passing two crossroads of tracks to continue down the cinder track to climb over a white-painted stile. Bear diagonally left to climb up to a kissing gate out of the horse paddocks. Cross the field then follow the left side of a hedgerow across a small open field and then continue along with the hedgerow to your right, towards the windmill. Please do not make a short cut across the private field, instead follow the hedgerow to the road of Lacey Green. Turn right past the bus stop and right again for the lane to the windmill or continue for 10 yards to the pub, The Whip Inn.

Lacey Green Windmill (SP819008)
This mill is the oldest smock mill in England, said to have been moved here from Chesham in 1821; the brick base is early 19th century. Pevsner describes this windmill as a timber-framed and weather-boarded smock mill of 1650, strengthened and given a new weather-boarded outer skin, sails and fantail by the Chiltern Society in the 1970s. In 1993, a spokesman from the Chiltern Society told us, a 'sheaf to loaf' competition was held. The challenge was to make a loaf within an hour of the grain being on the stalk. The army set up a field kitchen near the mill, and sure enough a loaf was milled and baked within the hour!

Open Sundays and BHs 2–5. www.laceygreenwindmill.org.uk

Access Point: Lacey Green, The Whip Inn, 5.5 miles. Pub, limited car parking, buses. SP818007.

The curious name of The Whip Inn refers to the pub landlord (1976-1999) who was referred to as 'Dick The Whip' Williams, from fox-hunting days. The pub sign shows a stagecoach with the coachman whipping the horses.

Having visited the mill and pub we recommend taking the field route (Option B) back to Lily Bank Farm since Pink Road is narrow with fast traffic and no good road verges. So, from the road end of the track to the windmill, turn left and almost immediately left again (signposted 'Chiltern Way') through a kissing gate to follow the right side of the hedgerow (NE). Continue in the same direction through three more kissing gates before reaching horse paddocks. Bear diagonally right to a white-painted stile and turn left uphill on the cinder track. Keep in the same direction between the fences to reach a stile beside a metal gate, then go diagonally right (NE, 45°) under the pylon to a stile on the far side of the field to descend bearing right (E) into the woodland. Turn left down the bridleway to Lily Bank Farm. At the farm buildings turn left (NW) to follow Lily Bottom Lane to the Pink and Lily pub on the left.

Access point: Parslow's Hillock parking in the pub car park for patrons only. SP827018.

If not visiting the pub, cross the road with great care towards the road opposite, Wardrobes Lane (so called after the large house at the bottom of the hill). Here turn right along the NW verge. Go for 50 yards, and at the sharp right hand turn of the road, turn left by the bungalow 'Little Woodlands'. Follow the right of two bridleways by turning right through the gate to continue through the wood (NE, 23°) for 0.5 miles. This track follows a small section of Black Hedge, a blackthorn hedge dating back to Anglo-Saxon times.

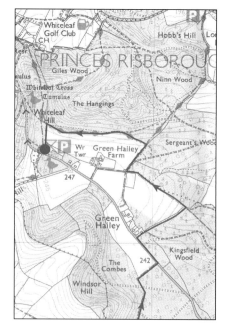

The Pink and Lily pub

When we first walked this route we could not understand why there was first Lily Bank Farm, then Pink Road and now the Pink and Lily pub. The history describes how a family home was changed to a hostelry in the early 1800s when two employees of the local Hampden family were in a predicament. Mr Pink was the butler at Hampden House and Miss Lillie a chambermaid, pregnant with his baby out of wedlock. They were sacked and forced to move out of 'The Big House' and set up this hostelry which still bears their names.

The famous war poet Rupert Brooke, author of 'The Soldier' with its opening *"If I should die think only this of me, There is some corner of a foreign field, That is forever England"*, regularly walked the Chiltern Hills and drank in the snug in this pub where there is his self-portrait and a book of his poems. The snug has remained much unchanged with a drying rack for sides of bacon.

Where a track crosses east-west, keep ahead (NW) to go to the fence along the edge of the wood and turn right (NE) alongside the field. At the road, turn left (NW) and follow it for 250 yards, taking care of the fast traffic. Beside the road are fine examples of native trees with coppiced hazel, and woodland banks. Pass the first (private) track on the right but turn right at a red letterbox to go down the house drive to Peppercorn Cottage. At the waymark sign keep ahead, then once into the wood, at the division of tracks, bear left (NE, 172°) to keep parallel to the left (NW) edge of the wood.

Autumnal woodland colours

Even though it was November when we walked through this wood, there was a vivid array of leaf colour: pale lemon of the near-circular hazel leaves; darker yellow of the wild raspberries; a pale scarlet of the blackberries; the copper leaves of the occasional larch tree and the palest of apple-green of the wild clematis.

On reaching the coniferous plantation, turn left (NW, 315°) onto a bridleway along the edge of a wood climbing gently on the chalky soil to reach a crossing of paths by a shed and a satellite dish. Turn right (NE) to follow the left (NW) side of Sergeant's Wood to turn left (W) still on the edge of the wood. Follow the south side of The Hangings, a reference to the Old English *hangra* 'a slope', the name for wood on a steep slope (*see Pitstone walk, p.122*), to meet the broad track of The Ridgeway. Turn left (S) for 120 yards past the practice trenches on the left, bearing left for another 100 yards to return to the car park.

Mapledurham

Start and finish point SU646820

Our route descends from Woodcote village through beech woods to Nuney Green and down the steep chalk slope of the River Thames valley. The tall chimneys of Mapledurham House can be seen as we descend. The 15th-century watermill is the only working one on the Thames. We return via the wild woods behind Hardwick House, the inspiration for Toad Hall in The Wind in the Willows. We cross Whitchurch Hill to return to Woodcote.

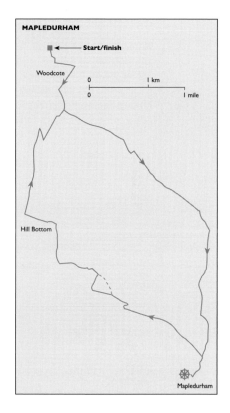

Distance: 9.8 miles (15.7 km).

Maps: Explorer 171 – Chiltern Hills West.
Landranger 175 – Reading, Windsor & surrounding area.

Transport: Buses   • Reading–Oxford via Chazey Heath (3 miles from Mapledurham) and Woodcote X39/X40. www.thames-travel.co.uk
     • Reading–Checkendon (for Hill Bottom). Thames Travel 142.

Taxis: Goring Heath   • Chrissie's Cabs. Tel: 01491 682412.
             Goring   • Golden Taxis. Tel: 01491 871111.

Car Parking: Woodcote Village Hall car park SU646820 (RG8 0QY).

Accommodation/Public Houses/Refreshments:
             Woodcote   • Red Lion PH, Goring Road. Tel: 01491 680483.
                            • Black Lion, Greenmoor Hill. (Light snacks only).
                              Tel: 01491 680625.
                            • The Woody Nook, B&B. Weds–Sats inclusive.
                              Tel: 01491 680775.
             Mapledurham   • Mapledurham House. (Refreshments) Tel: 01189 723350.
             Hill Bottom   • The Sun Inn. Tel: 01189 842260.
             Goring Heath   • Blackbirds Cottage. (1.2 miles from route).
                              Tel: 01491 681760.
             Chazey Heath   • JoeDaisy Guest House. (On bus route, 3.5 miles from
                              walk). Tel: 01189 483155. www.joedaisyguesthouse.co.uk

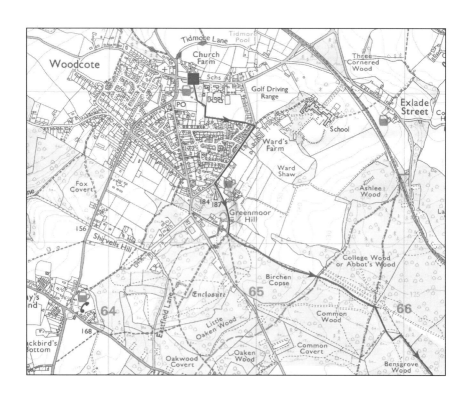

From the village hall walk diagonally left across the village green (SE, 143°) to the far side, to leave via a metal kissing gate. Follow the narrow footpath behind the houses (E), cross a road to continue through the housing estate to arrive at the road (Greenmoor), turn right along this road (SW) as far as the Black Lion pub. At the pub turn left (SE) onto a tarmac bridleway passing the telecommunications tower to the right on Greenmoor Hill.

It is worth pausing at Greenmoor Hill Farm on the left side to admire the view across the woodlands to the south towards London. A local person said that, on a clear day, it is possible to see Windsor Castle and the top of the new Ascot racecourse grandstand left (E) of the grey office blocks at Bracknell. We watched aeroplanes climbing steeply as they took off from Heathrow Airport 23 miles away.

Descend a gravel drive (S, 170°) as far as a house called 'Trees', and turn left. Enter the beech woods taking the left fork of three paths, to gently descend the northern edge of the wood (SE) through Birchen Copse for over 750 yards, to reach a waymark of three arrows where there is a crossing path. Go over the pair of railway sleepers and continue in the same direction still following the white arrows for 450 yards, keeping parallel with a long, moss-covered, ancient woodland bank to the left. (Although there are two banks shown on the map, we could only see one). On reaching the second three-arrow waymark and a crossing path, keep ahead by going left around a holly tree to a hidden path beyond it, still going in the same direction (SE, 130°). *Do not* bear right on the waymarked path beside a wire fence. Continue to follow the bridleway (SE) passing an orange-topped post (SE) on your right. Walk for nearly half a mile in the same direction (SE) through Bensgrove Wood to arrive at the road called Deadman's Lane. Lanes so-named were often former ways along which coffins were carried from scattered hamlets to the parish church. Cross the lane onto a bridleway marked 'Nuney Green ¾' climbing gently through a wood called The Hocket (Old English *hoc* 'projecting corner') and along the edge of Hawhill Wood.

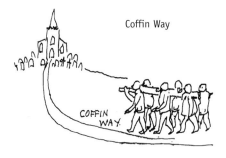

Coffin Way

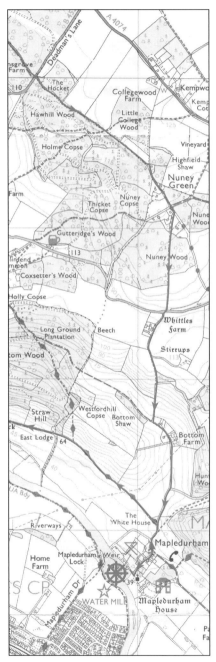

There are more woodland banks here which were built in medieval times to keep the deer out of the wood, since this was the place where hazel trees were coppiced and used for fencing. Large trees grown as 'standards' for the timber were used in building construction.

Continue alongside the edge of the wood (SE), but at a stile at the next fork, take the right path beside a wire fence on your left. At another fork in the paths bear left (135°), not on the path with the green notice and welcome sign, but keeping close to the long rectangular clearing on the left marked on the map. At the woodland pond on the right, follow the arrows around the left side of it. Leave the wood passing one of the crofter's cottages on the right side, into the hamlet of **Nuney Green**.

Tucked behind the hedge on the left is a house called Kinoull, which is worth pausing to look at. It has a long low thatched roof with three thatched dormers known colloquially as 'eyebrows'.

An example of thatched 'eyebrows'

Nuney Green is a good example of a dispersed woodland settlement from medieval times, rather than the clustered villages of arable lowland. Continue along a gravel road (SE), but where the road turns right take the footpath ahead for only 50 yards before bearing right on a footpath marked 'Mapledurham 1½'.

One of the 16th-century crofter's cottages is on the right, with a corrugated iron roof replacing the original thatch. It is however still single storey with a large central chimney stack. You can imagine that the Hansel and Gretel's woodcutter's cottage was like this!

Descend along a sunken way (S) through Nuney Wood, and out through a kissing gate into a field to walk down beside a line of trees keeping near to the fence. Cross the road to turn right and then left, signed 'Mapledurham 1', to go up a track towards Whittles Farm. Pevsner describes this farmhouse, dating from the 14th century. It is L-shaped, timber framed, and the walls built of brick and flint. Follow the track, but where it curves left towards another ancient building (Stirrups) go through a wooden kissing gate on the right (easily missed), to descend the hill on the right side of the hedge, to the bottom. There is a magnificent view down to the village of Mapledurham, the huge manor house with its tall chimneys and its church. Beyond are the River Thames, the railway and the woodlands stretching towards Caversham. The white building on the horizon is a water tower. Follow the path with a multi-specied hedge on the left and a newly planted orchard to the right.

When we walked in October the spindle bushes were full of pink berries, the blackthorn hung with blue sloes and the purging buckthorn bushes with small black berries. A purgative was made from the bark and fruit of this shrub, and also a sap-green pigment from the berries. Wild marjoram and the blue clustered bellflower grow on the chalky soil.

Purging buckthorn

In the base of the valley turn left, first passing Bottom Farm Cottages, then the farm buildings, which include a half-timbered granary store on staddle stones (*see Brill walk, p.29*) and a flint barn. It was interesting that the barn walls were built only of flint with the more solid brick quoins at the corners to give it strength. At the road turn right into the hamlet of **Mapledurham**, taking great care of the traffic. The houses are again a mixture of brick and flint. The house on the left dates from 1691 and the almshouses on the right are also 17th-century. Continue to the church.

Mapledurham Estate (SU668767)

Mapledurhan House

Mapledurham House
The Catholic Blount family have owned the Mapledurham estate for the last 500 years. The fine Elizabethan house was built in the traditional 'E' shape to show the family's allegiance to the Queen. The front faces eastwards rather than towards the river since in those times people dreaded the miasma (river mists). There is a long vista with a ha-ha to ensure an unbroken view. The modern gates on the church side have pomegranate gate finials, with one of the pomegranates having a slice out of it!

St Margaret's Church
The 14th-century church is remarkable as it has a separate Roman Catholic chapel within a Church of England building. The Blount monument of Robert Bardolf and his wife shows the knight in armour and his lady with exaggerated coiffure, farthingale and ruff. The font is older than the church, being Norman with a diagonal raised pattern.

Mapledurham Estate *(contd.)*

Mapledurham Watermill (SU669768)
The 15th-century watermill is now the last working corn and grist mill on the River Thames. A grist mill was a mill to which farmers brought their own grain and received back ground meal or flour, minus a percentage called the 'miller's toll'. The Great Plague of 1677 meant that the Royal Court was moved to Abingdon and the millers of Mapledurham were ready to profit from this new source of business.

It was featured in the film *The Eagle has Landed*, with Michael Caine in the star role. In the film the mill was blown up, but in fact it was a modern replica built near the old mill!

A modern source of power is the Archimedes screw turbine beside the old mill. It generates 500,000 kWh of green electricity per annum, sufficient to fuel 140 houses a year.

The waterwheel

Admission details and opening times for the Mapledurham Estate
Opening times: Mill summer openings: Saturdays, Sundays, and BH Mondays. Teas. 2–5. Admission: House & Mill: £9.50 (Seniors £8.00). Winter openings: watermill and shop for flour 1st and 3rd Sundays. 10–1.
For details of opening times please go to: www.mapledurham.co.uk; contact: enquiries@mapledurham.co.uk or Tel: 01189 723350.

NB there is plentiful car parking provision while the house and mill are open, but none when they are closed. This restriction protects this secluded hamlet. If wanting to visit both the house and mill in the summer, it is best not to leave Woodcote until 11am to avoid arriving too early.

Retrace your steps from the village along the road for 400 yards to turn left along a bridleway marked 'Whitchurch 2½ miles' just before The White House marked on the map. Follow this narrow track parallel to the River Thames past more spindle bushes. It is worth stopping to look back to see the weir on the Thames at Mapledurham Lock and to see the walkers following the Thames Path on the other river bank. Ignore a footpath leaving on the right, but continue to the elaborate wrought iron gates of the East Lodge of Hardwick House. Continue along the bridleway behind the house. At the notice saying 'Private Drive', is our only chance to see part of Hardwick House (a good view can be obtained from the footpath on the opposite (S) bank of the Thames). Follow the track past the hedges at the back of the house.

Hardwick House

The house was the inspiration for Toad Hall from Kenneth Grahame's 1908 children's classic, *The Wind in the Willows*. We can, however, walk through what Grahame calls the Wild Wood. This is Mole's first experience of it:

'There was nothing to alarm him at first entry. Twigs crackled under his feet, logs tripped him, funguses on stumps resembled caricatures, and startled him for the moment by their likeness to something familiar and far away... Then the faces began. It was over his shoulder, and indistinctly, that he first thought he saw a face: a little evil wedge-shaped face, looking out at him from a hole.'

At a crossing of paths, and just past the notice of the Hardwick Estate Office, turn right up a stony track into the woods. Bear right following this track, to then sweep round left to ascend through the woods (NW). At a fork, keep left (W, 270°) on a level permissive path, passing what looks like either the remains of an air-raid shelter or lime kiln in a hollow on the right. This is known locally as 'the Bear Pit' and its origin is a mystery.

Short cut

There is an option for a short cut here by following the uphill path (NW), which leads into the lane to Path Hill Farm, where the main route joins.

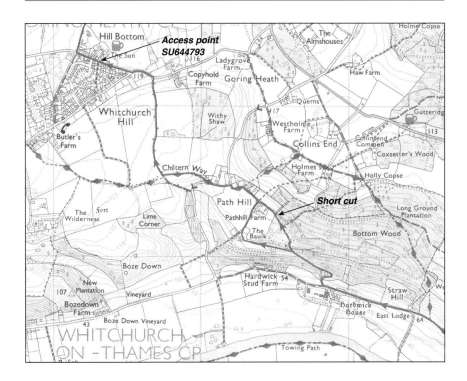

On the level path, at a wooden barrier, bear left down the footpath, as it descends the slope for a short while, to keep travelling west. At the junction of paths just after the remarkable flintwork house called The Baulk (Old English 'a bank'), turn right uphill to pass the house on the right. Follow the drive to reach Path Hill Farm (an outdoor centre). Here, over the gate opposite, it is possible to see the telecommunications tower (N) on Greenmoor Hill near our starting point. Do not follow the footpath through the gate, but turn left (NW) along the lane,

The Baulk

ignoring a Chilterns Way footpath sign to the right. Beware of traffic. The hamlet of **Path Hill** is another example of a scattered woodland settlement. Where the lane meets a road, turn sharp left, past the few houses, for about 200 yards to the end of the houses. Leave the road by taking a footpath labelled 'Whitchurch Hill ¾' on the right (part of the Chilterns Way extension). Follow the enclosed path, through a kissing gate and beside the hedgerow along the upper side of the field to another kissing gate. Turn right (N) onto a track (a RUPP i.e. a road used as a public path) across Whitchurch Hill. Turn left at the road and at the fork bear right into the village of **Hill Bottom**, passing The Sun Inn.

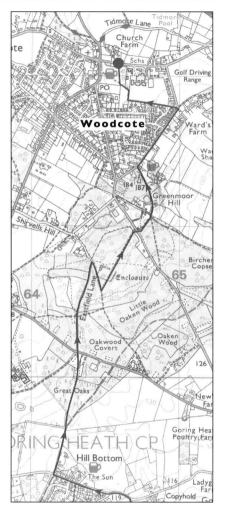

Access Point: Hill Bottom 7.4 miles. Pub, bus. SU644793.

Where the houses end, turn right (N) onto a bridleway (Gashes Lane) to enter a wood. At an old trailer, bear left onto a footpath (N) (not the bridleway leading NE) to go into a wood called Great Oaks. Continue ahead to go through the wood to where a path crosses in front of a builder's yard. Turn left here and right after 100 yards to follow the diverted path to the road. Cross the road (Deadman's Lane) onto a wide track opposite called Eastfield Lane. Continue (N) for 650 yards to where the lane veers left and there is a prominent footpath sign on the right where we have to double back for 190 yards (see map). The point of doubling back (SE) is at the white painted arrows on a tree trunk. It is clearly marked at the junction, so turn left (NE) to follow the white painted arrows. When you see a wire fence with a small wooden gate in it, follow the fence NE to meet a road at a converted Primitive Methodist Chapel dated 1886. Turn left uphill for 100 yards on the road taking great care, then turn right before the 30 mile restriction sign, onto a bridleway to follow a garden fence on the right to a path junction. Turn right (SE) on the bridleway at a black and white timbered house, to turn left (N) at the house called 'Trees' that we passed on the outward journey. Climb the bridleway again passing the panoramic viewpoint of our outward route. Turn right at the end of the drive, passing the Black Lion pub on the edge of **Woodcote**, to follow the road (NE) for 800 yards until a left-hand bend. Then at the footpath sign go left through the housing estate and return along the enclosed path to turn right (NW) at the kissing gate and back to the village hall car park.

Tower and Smock Mills

By the 15th century post mills had begun to be superseded by tower mills which were constructed as a circular tower, usually of stone or brick, containing the machinery on a number of floors. The crucial advantage of tower mills was that only the cap, with the sails attached, rotated, rather than the whole body of the mill. These mills met the need for larger and more stable sources of power in the growing economy. As only the cap of the tower needed turning, the main structure could be made taller, allowing the miller to unreef sails. This resulted in useful work in low winds. The cap could be rotated either by winches inside the cap or from a winch on the tail pole outside the mill (*see Pitstone windmill, p.127*). Later in the mid 18th century the task was automated by fitting a fan tail (a small windmill mounted at right angles to the sails, at the rear of the windmill (*see Great Haseley windmill, p.91*).

The smock mill is a later variation of the tower mill where the tower is replaced by a wooden octagonal structure called the 'smock', the name arising from its shape resembling a peasant's smock.

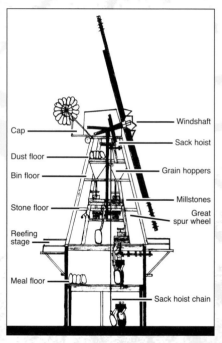

Diagram of a Tower Mill

Smock   Smock Mill

Pitstone

Start and finish point SP943163

This walk is based on the Buckinghamshire/Hertfordshire borders. We start from Ivinghoe village on the Lower Icknield Way with an opportunity to climb to the top of Ivinghoe Beacon, a chalk outlier of the Chiltern Hills. The route follows the scarp edge though the beechwoods of the Ashridge estate and descends into the picturesque village of Aldbury. We return over the downland to pass England's oldest windmill near Pitstone, and on through Ivinghoe village to reach the Ford End watermill.

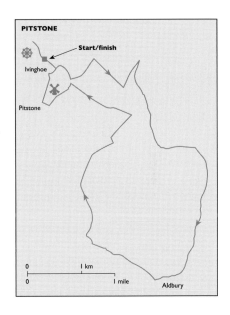

Distance: 10.4 miles (16.7 km) with ascent to Ivinghoe Beacon, 9.4 miles (15 km) without.

Maps: Explorer 181 – Chiltern Hills North.
Landranger 165 – Aylesbury, Leighton Buzzard.

Transport: Buses
- Ivinghoe. Arriva 61. Traveline Tel: 08712 002233.
- Aylesbury and Tring. Redline buses 164. (Mon–Sat only). Tel: 01296 426786.
- Aldbury. Arriva 30/31, 387, or Chiltern Rambler 327. (Sundays only, May–September). Centrebus, Tel: 0870 444746.

Rail
- Cheddington Station (2.2miles NW of Ivinghoe village, SP922185).
- Tring Station (1.1 miles W of Aldbury, SP951122).

• Frequent London Midland services from Euston and Birmingham.

Taxis: Cheddington   • Cheddington Cars. Tel: 01296 661666.
            Tring   • John Taxis. Tel: 01442 828828.
                    • EcoCabs2Go. Tel: 01296 661999.

Car Parking: Station Road, Ivinghoe near the entrance of Ladysmith Road (NW corner of the village green) SP943163 (LU7 9EB).

Accommodation/Public Houses/Refreshments:
Aldbury   • The Greyhound Inn. Tel: 01442 851228.
            www.greyhoundaldbury.co.uk
        • The Valiant Trooper. Tel: 01442 851203.
            www.valianttrooper.co.uk
Ivinghoe   • The King's Head. Tel: 01296 668388.
            www.kingsheadivinghoe.co.uk
        • The Rose and Crown. Tel: 01296 668472.
            www.roseandcrownivinghoe.com
        • CuriosiTEA Tea Rooms, Old School Community Yard.
            Tel: 07775 831153. Open weekdays 9–4.30
            (Wednesdays 9–2); weekends 10–3.
        • Town Farm Camping. Tel: 01296 668455.
            www.townfarmcamping.co.uk

Ivinghoe village
It is said that Sir Walter Scott named his novel 'Ivanhoe' after this village. The village street lies on the route of the Lower Icknield Way, a Bronze Age trackway from Norfolk to Dorset. The Upper Icknield Way is on the slightly higher land which the B489 towards Dunstable follows. This now small village was originally a market town, however, by the mid 16th century it began to lose trade to Tring (Herts) and Dunstable (Beds). By the early 19th century the market was dying and the main occupation was straw plaiting for hats, controlled from Luton and Dunstable.

From Station Road, go uphill alongside the village green, towards the King's Head inn. At the corner turn left (NE) along Church Street (the Lower Icknield Way) passing the Old Vicarage on the left. Continue on the narrow footpath for 250 yards to leave the village, taking great care of the traffic. At the junction signposted 'Dunstable and Ashridge', turn left (NE) onto the B489 (the Upper Icknield Way) to again keep to the footpath beside the busy road as far as Town Farm.

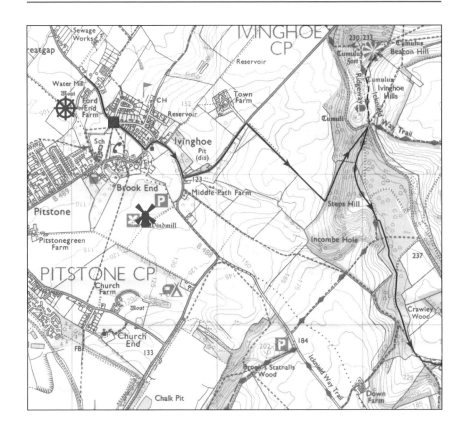

St Mary's Church, Ivinghoe

St Mary's Church (originally 13th century) is a light-filled, cruciform building of the local knapped flint with a Hertfordshire flèche. A flèche is a lead-covered needle-like spire and is always called 'Hertfordshire' regardless of the county it is in. The stone capitals are built of local Tottenhoe stone (a hard chalk) with ballflower decoration on the doorway of the porch. The wooden roof is particularly fine and has carved angels with outspread wings. One of the carvings on the medieval poppyhead pew-ends is of a mermaid complete with a square comb and mirror! (Find her behind the third column from the altar in the south aisle). Mermaids are widely found in medieval churches as warnings against vanity and lust! On the exterior wall near the gate is a large hook that was used for pulling thatch off burning buildings. There is an opportunity to explore the village at the end of the walk.

At Town Farm, turn right (SE) onto a footpath following the right side of the remains of an old hedgeline and continuing SE to the fenceline at the base of the escarpment (Steps Hill). Go through the gate and turn left (NE) beside the wire fence and over a stile. Bear right and climb gently between the bushes up to the road at the base of Ivinghoe Beacon. Turn right to walk beside the road for 40 yards. Here there is an optional 0.7 mile diversion of climbing the Beacon. Otherwise, if you decide not to climb Beacon Hill, turn right (S) off the road to follow the Ridgeway.

Ivinghoe Beacon

Ivinghoe Beacon marks the end of the Chiltern scarp edge. It is 764 feet (233 metres) high and has an Iron Age hill fort and a tumulus on its summit dating from c.750 BC. The ramparts of the hill fort can be seen on the right side of the Beacon. As you climb the slope you will notice that this is an area of unimproved chalk grassland, with blue scabious, deep crimson salad burnet flowers and marbled white and chalkhill blue butterflies.

Diversion to Ivinghoe Beacon

To reach the top of the Beacon take the left hand path directly uphill, marked 'Ivinghoe Beacon ½ mile', following the white acorn signs of The Ridgeway National Trail. Alternatively, for a more gentle ascent (1.1 miles), bear right along the paths up the side of the Beacon towards Gallows Hill and then turn left to approach the summit from the east. From the top of the Beacon it is possible to see Mentmore Towers (NW), a large pale-coloured building built for Baron de Rothschild, described as one of the greatest houses of the Victorian era. Other landmarks include Waddesdon Hill (W), on which Waddesdon Manor lies, and the bridge where the Great Train Robbery took place. Retrace your steps down the steep side of the Beacon or via the more gentle route down towards Gallows Hill and back to the starting place by the road. If returning from the Beacon diversion, cross the road with great care.

Keep to the acorn markers uphill (S) between the bushes for about 50 yards, then bear right (SW, 220°) onwards to go through a gate where there is a brown sign for the Ashridge Boundary Trail.

The Great Train Robbery — August 8th 1963
This infamous robbery of £2.6 million (now the equivalent of £50 million) of used bank notes in postal sacks on board the night mail train from Glasgow, is thought to be the largest ever made. The 15-strong gang established their base at Leatherslade Farm (SP625120) 1 mile south of Brill in Oxfordshire (*see Brill walk, p.25*). They committed the robbery at Bridego railway bridge, near Ledburn, Leighton Buzzard near the B4488 road leading north of Ivinghoe village. From the summit of the Beacon, to spot the bridge (SP916209) 3½ miles away, look (NW, 310°) and follow with your eye the hedgerow that goes towards a farm, and beyond in the same direction to the bridge east of Horton Wharf. The pale-grey railway gantries are a good landmark.

Walk immediately left uphill beside a wire fence, ignoring the stile on the left, through more bushes and a narrow kissing gate to the top of a grassy slope where there is an Ashridge Estate sign and a noticeboard (titled 'The Hills Are Alive') which explains the management of the landscape. Continue (S) past the noticeboard along the open chalk grassland, keeping above the steep-sided combe (Incombe Hole) down on the right, to continue along the Ridgeway for a further 80 yards only (and not down into the open fields) before going through a gate on your left. Double back five yards, and then follow the track to the right (SE) through the woods to go through a gate beside a cattle grid. You are now in the beech-woods of the Ashridge Estate. Follow the wide gravel track (S) under a canopy of mature beech trees. Where the tracks divide, keep

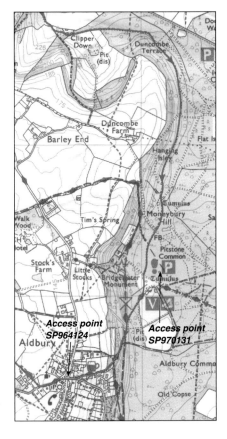

left on the Ashridge Cycle Route, and continue (E) towards the entrance of Clipper Down Cottage (kennels). Pass the waymark right of the cottage to follow the route (E) adjacent to the house and kennels. Continue walking down the dip slope in the beech woods for ½ mile.

When we walked through in April there was a carpet of bluebells and young bracken growing.

Pass the first carved log bench, then at the second carved bench there are the first views of the dry valley on the right in which Aldbury village is situated. The buildings of Duncombe Farm can be seen. A combe is the ancient English term for a steep-sided valley. Our route (S) keeps high along the contours through these beech hangers, hence the place name 'Hanging Isley' on the map. Where the track divides, keep following the Ashridge Cycle Route (SW) to go past a wooden building (a former Scout hut) on the right and a tumulus (an ancient burial mound). Continue on towards Moneybury Hill with its barrow, and the Bridgewater Monument.

The Ashridge Estate and the Father of Inland Waterways

The Ashridge Estate was established in the 13th century when a monastery was built by Edmund Plantagenet, Earl of Cornwall and nephew of King Henry III. Ashridge was then owned by Edward the Black Prince, and he established Ashridge as a place of pilgrimage. Due to the attractiveness of the building and the wider estate, King Henry VIII spared Ashridge during the dissolution of the monasteries. The estate was bequeathed to Princess Elizabeth who was arrested at Ashridge on the orders of her sister Mary Tudor. The straight wide ride (SW) is known as Prince's Riding. In 1604 the estates was purchased by the Egerton family. It was Francis Egerton, third Duke of Bridgewater, who was nicknamed 'The Canal Duke', who revolutionised canal transport, after successfully building a canal opened in 1761, to connect the coal mines in Worsley, west of Manchester, to the industrial centres of the North West. He was the first person to ignore existing river courses by creating 'The Duke's Cut'. His initiatives started 'the golden canal era' which resulted in a halving of the price of coal since it could be transported to cities much more efficiently than by horse and cart. One barge horse could pull 20–30 tonnes of goods.

From the top of the Bridgewater Monument (33 metres high) it is possible to see seven counties on a clear day, including Cambridgeshire, and Canary Wharf and Wembley Stadium in Greater London.

Tel: 01442 850004. www.ashridgenationaltrust.org.uk

Access Point: Bridgewater monument, 4.7 miles. Car parking, café, toilets and shop. SP970131.

Pass the monument and at the small white cottage with a central chimney (the café), bear right (SW) along the stony track into the woods to descend the Ashridge Boundary Trail. At the point where the trail splits, bear right, ignoring Meadow Trail, which continues along the top of the slope, and instead follow Old Copse Trail to descend the slope. Continue for 100 yards to the two brown signs, bearing right at a sign 'No Mobility Vehicles', into a sunken way with its steep chalk sides, always keeping to the main path. This is the steep scarp slope of the Chilterns and it is possible to see the village of **Aldbury** down below through the trees. At the bottom,

Bridgewater Monument

the slope flattens out and enters the village joining one of the main village roads. Turn right towards the centre of Aldbury and continue (W) past the village pond to Station Road.

Access Point: Aldbury village centre, 5.3 miles. Limited parking, pubs, shop, buses. (Tring Station 1 mile by road). SP964124.

Leave the village along Station Road (SW) beside the church (*see following page*) to turn right (NW) just past the churchyard onto a footpath signed 'Pitstone Hill 1½ miles'. Keep right of Church Farm on the left but keep close to the farm buildings to go left and right through a small gate beside a barn wall.

House martins were sweeping into the barn enclosure in May.

Continue (NW) along an enclosed path to keep going in the same direction at the point where a bridleway crosses. Cross the bridleway and climb up (NW) across the golf course.

Aldbury

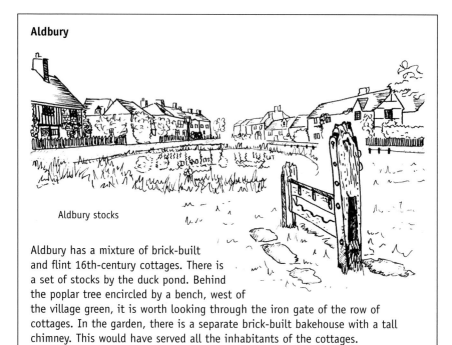

Aldbury stocks

Aldbury has a mixture of brick-built
and flint 16th-century cottages. There is
a set of stocks by the duck pond. Behind
the poplar tree encircled by a bench, west of
the village green, it is worth looking through the iron gate of the row of
cottages. In the garden, there is a separate brick-built bakehouse with a tall
chimney. This would have served all the inhabitants of the cottages.

Inside the flint-built church of St John the Baptist is the Pendley Chapel,
with a rare stone screen enclosing the monuments. These include the tomb
of Sir Robert Whittingham who was slain at the battle of Tewkesbury in 1471
during the Wars of the Roses. At his feet is a Wild Man of the Woods or
woodwose, representing the animal side of man
or a romantic allusion to Nature.

Woodwose

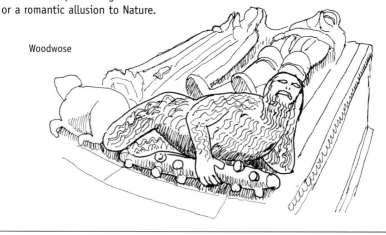

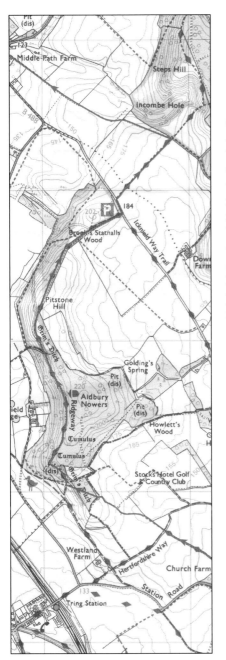

We noticed an unusual green-painted metal post with a towel. This is a Par Aide ball washer, a device to clean golf balls so that a low score (par) is achieved!

Further up the slope, go through a small gate into the woods of Aldbury Nowers. The place name 'Nowers' means 'on or at the foot of a hill slope'. Follow the path through the woods and on reaching a crossing path dogleg left and right across the line of Grim's Ditch, a long linear earthwork. Go up the wooden steps and immediately fork left, once again on the Ridgeway path. You will shortly pass the Aldbury Nowers nature reserve.

Marbled white butterfly which breed at the Aldbury Nowers Nature Reserve

Aldbury Nowers Nature Reserve (SP950132)
This is a Site of Special Scientific Interest where wild thyme, cowslips, clustered bell flowers, violets, wild marjoram, small scabious, rock rose, milkwort, and wild strawberry grow on the unimproved chalk grassland. The wild thyme favours the well-drained soil thrown up by ants' nests. There is a different ecology of plants growing on the windward and leeward sides of anthills. This is also one of the best sites for butterflies in Hertfordshire: the 30 species of butterfly breeding here include marbled white, green hairstreak, brown argus, both grizzled and dingy skippers. There have been sightings of the rare Duke of Burgundy.

Wild strawberry

www.hertswildlifetrust.org.uk/NatureReserves/Local/aldburynowers

Keep following the Ridgeway (N) to go out into the open downland, over the crossroads of paths to pass the ramparts of an Iron Age hillfort on the right with views of the chalk extraction at Pitstone Quarry to the north west. Follow the contours (NE) to cross a footpath keeping near the wire fences to go towards the right of Pitstone Hill. Near a road, an information board explains the landscape. Dogleg left (NW) and then right through the car park to arrive at a minor road.

Cross the road to follow the Ridgeway path (NE) opposite. At a crossing path below the steep slopes of Incombe Hole (*see map*), turn left (NW) at a waymark post signed 'Ivinghoe 1 mile' to leave the Ridgeway path. Follow the remains of the hedgerow aiming for the church tower in Ivinghoe.

We heard the call of the green woodpecker on these grassy slopes.

Go through the wide field gates, bear slightly to the left and keep in the same direction (NW) across an open field, then along the left side of a hedgerow. Go through a gate and along an enclosed path in the same direction. On arriving at a gate onto the road, turn left (S) to keep on the verge for safety. We suggest walking on beyond the entrance to the windmill for at least 75 yards, crossing over where the road straightens, to get a better view of oncoming traffic. To reach the windmill take the track (SW).

Access Point: Pitstone Windmill 8.8 miles. Limited parking. SP947158.

Pitstone windmill (SP945157)

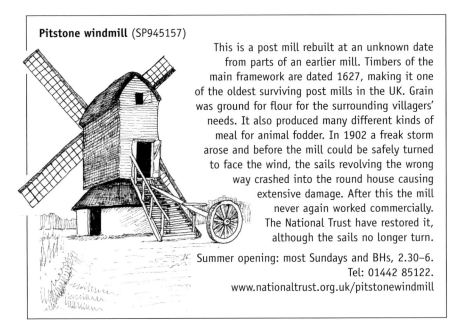

This is a post mill rebuilt at an unknown date from parts of an earlier mill. Timbers of the main framework are dated 1627, making it one of the oldest surviving post mills in the UK. Grain was ground for flour for the surrounding villagers' needs. It also produced many different kinds of meal for animal fodder. In 1902 a freak storm arose and before the mill could be safely turned to face the wind, the sails revolving the wrong way crashed into the round house causing extensive damage. After this the mill never again worked commercially. The National Trust have restored it, although the sails no longer turn.

Summer opening: most Sundays and BHs, 2.30–6.
Tel: 01442 85122.
www.nationaltrust.org.uk/pitstonewindmill

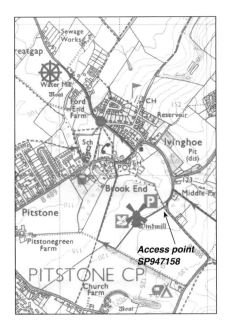

Beyond the windmill continue on the track (SW) to turn right (NW) beside the wood. Fifty yards beyond the edge of the wood, turn right again (NE) on the footpath across the middle of the field, aiming left of **Ivinghoe** church tower. Go through a gate, along an enclosed path up Green Lane to the village street. Here turn right (E) along the street, which has brick-and-timbered houses, passing the tea rooms in the old school on the left.

On arriving at the village green, the former Brewery House, a tall red brick, elegant building built about 1800, and more recently a Youth Hostel, is on the right.

The King's Head pub (16th–17th century) is to the left, and beyond it is the church. To reach the Rose and Crown pub (also serving teas), keep along Church Street (NE), passing the Old Vicarage on the left, to turn left along Vicarage Road to the pub and the car parking area. To visit the Ford End watermill follow Station Road (NW) out of the village for 500 yards. The mill is on the left.

Ford End Watermill (SP941166)
This was a small farmer's mill typical of many such mills in the Chilterns. It is sited on a small stream, Whistle Brook, formed by surface water arising from springs below the chalk. It has a fall of 10 feet. The mill pond lies behind the buildings. It is thought to have been built on the site of a 13th-century mill, but officially recorded in 1616 and in use until 1963. It has now been restored to a working condition and stone-ground flour is on sale. It is the only remaining water mill in Buckinghamshire with most of its original machinery.

Open Sundays and BHs, April–September, 2–5 (last entry at 4.30).
Tel: 01442 825421. www.fordendwatermill.co.uk

Quainton

Start and finish point SP747202

Starting from Quainton windmill, the tallest in Buckinghamshire and with a climb to the highest hill in the district, we travel on the Midshires Way and the North Bucks Way to East Claydon. There is an optional diversion to the grand Palladian house at Middle Claydon, where Florence Nightingale stayed. We return to Quainton via Botolph Claydon going along Three Points Lane beside a part of the ancient Bernwood Forest.

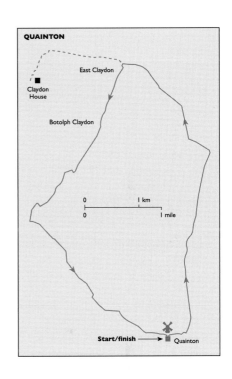

QUAINTON

East Claydon

Claydon House

Botolph Claydon

0   1 km
0   1 mile

Start/finish ⟶ Quainton

Distance: 9.2 miles (14.8 km), including diversion to Claydon House 11.9 miles (19.2 km).

Maps: Explorer 192 – Buckingham & Milton Keynes.
Explorer 181 – Chiltern Hills North.
Landranger 165 – Aylesbury & Leighton Buzzard.

Transport: Buses   • Red Rose 16. Aylesbury, Quainton, Waddesdon.

Taxis: Aylesbury   • Call A Cab. Tel: 01296 580506.
Winslow   • Church St Cars. Tel: 01296 712121.

- PRS Cars. Tel: 01296 713795.
- Braziers. Tel: 01296 712201.

Car Parking: Upper Street, on the north side of the village green. SP747202 (HP22 4AR).

Accommodation/Public Houses/Refreshments:

Middle Claydon • Claydon House, The Courtyard Tearooms. Tel: 01296 730349. www.claydonestate.co.uk

Botolph   • Botolph Farmhouse, B&B. Tel: 01296 712640. Claydon   www.botolphfarm.co.uk

Quainton   • George and Dragon PH and café (serves breakfasts). Tel: 01296 655436. www.georgeanddragonquainton.co.uk

- Ye Swan and Castle PH, Lower St. Tel: 01296 655276.

Quainton

The village name probably originates from Queen Edith, wife of Edward the Confessor, who had a manor at Quainton. The old spelling was CWENE-TUN meaning Queen's Manor. The village centre is set around a triangular green with the base and shaft of a medieval preaching cross. On the north side of the green is Cross Farmhouse, built in 1723, with its elaborate coat of arms. Most of the buildings are constructed in local brick made from nearby clay, and are timbered with brick nogging infill.

Quainton Windmill (SP746202)

Quainton Windmill is a 6-storey, brick-built tower mill, the tallest in Buckinghamshire, built tall as it lies in the lee of Quainton Hill, the highest hill in Buckinghamshire. People may wonder why it was not built on the top of the hill, but it was simply because the miller did not own that field. It was built in 1832 and therefore incorporated all the latest technology, such as patent sails (these have automatically operated shutters, so are easier to operate than canvas sails). It was, however, built just before steam mills replaced the more unpredictable windmills. In 1896 the fantail blew off and the mill fell into ruin. Restoration started in 1976: at present the sails are being replaced and it should be back to its former glory shortly.

Windmill open April–October, Sundays, 10–1 or tours can booked in advance: enquiries to: info@quaintonwindmill.org.uk and www.quaintonwindmill.org.uk

Quainton windmill

From standing on the village green facing north towards the windmill, turn right (E) to the start of Church Street passing the noticeboard about Bernwood Forest. Do not take the footpath left, but continue along Church Street past the Village Store to enjoy the local timber-framed and brick buildings en route.

The first house after the windmill is jettied (with a wooden overhang) and the Village Store on the right has remarkably large ammonites set into the street wall.

Further on, are houses with 1722 fire insurance plaques. The curious name of the road on the right 'The Pyghtles' comes from the name given by the Church for a small parcel of land. On the left of this close is Banner Farmhouse, a good example of timber framing with brick herringbone nogging. Past Baker's Cottage at the end of the street are the Winwood Almshouses built, as a tribute in the church describes, 'for the support of six poor widows and widowers in the parish.' These impoverished people were also left a farm and grazing land to provide an income for their maintenance.

Ammonite in the wall of the village store

St Mary and Holy Cross Church

The church of St Mary and Holy Cross is a large church with some exceptionally rich 17th and 18th century monuments. In the west end of the south aisle, Sir Richard Winwood (builder of the almshouses and Principal Secretary of King James I) and his wife lie on a black tomb with a carved skeleton on the side. There are more remarkable monuments in the tower, but they are not normally viewable without an appointment.

For church keys contact Mr Campbell, Tel: 01296 655243,
Mrs Leeming, Tel: 01296 655342 or Jane Vowles, Tel: 01296 658665.

Continue past the church, and 150 yards further on, turn left over a stile onto 'Matthew's Way'. Go uphill across the small field, to cross double stiles in the middle of the hedge. Continue in the same direction (N, 20°) across the next field to pass near the protruding hedge corner to join a tarmac track and on to the right-hand end of the hedgerow ahead. At the next hedgerow turn left onto the Swans Way to turn right through a large metal gate on the bridleway. Aim for the telecommunications mast on the summit of Quainton Hill, by going uphill to another gate in the far hedgerow (N, 340°), up the next field past the trig point and reservoir and through the gap on the left (W) side of the mast. There are 360° views with Waddesdon Hill (S), the village of Whitchurch to the right (E), Arncott Hill, near Bicester (SW), and the Stokenchurch mast (S) on the Chiltern Hills ridge.

There was glorious silence up here apart from birdsong and the wind in the trees, but sadly this tranquillity is threatened by the route of the HS2 express train.

Go over the summit of the hill, and across the field beyond (N) on the bridleway to the large metal field gate then on (N) to the second metal gate (SP750217) at the end of the next field. From this gate bear slightly right (N, 10°) across the summit of the hill (be careful not to go left towards Hogshaw Hill Farm along the line of ash trees ahead). Descend the hill in the bottom of a shallow valley between two outcrops of orangey soil, with old railed horse jumps up to the right. Aim to the right of the large grey electricity sub-station using the landmark of the village of Granborough (SP768250) which has a square church tower (and is a smaller village than Hoggeston further to the right). Descend Conduit Hill (N, 27°), where the low red-brick farm building with a pond can be seen to the right of Fulbrook Farm on the low land ahead. A closer landmark, at the base of the hill, is the muddy hedgerow gap with a metal gate where the bridleway goes. Those with binoculars will be able to see, in the fields beyond, the metal kissing gate beside the lane which is on our route. Go through the small gate right of this gap and across the next field (N), passing Fulbrook Farm to the left, through the line of a former hedgerow, across the second field to reach double metal kissing gates on either side of a small road at SP752226. The earthworks marked on the map surrounded a medieval manor at Fulbrook. The now deserted medieval village, just left of the footpath, is likely to have been situated here to utilise the numerous springs on the north side of Conduit Hill.

On the other side of the road, follow the marker (NNE, 50°) on the North Bucks Way along a well-marked path through the first two fields. At the wide hedge gap at the end of the third field bear right to the far right-hand corner of the field. At the end of this field (4th) go over a footbridge and stile and again bear right (NE, 18°) to the far right field corner. Go over a stile and footbridge in this corner, turn left on an enclosed path to cross another footbridge out onto a track. Turn left through a metal gate and onto the road and go left again (NW). Walk for 600 yards to where the entrance of Lower Farm meets the road on the left. Here turn right (NNW) through a gateway. In the field, continue (NW, 350°) staying parallel to the right-hand hedgerow to the far end of the field, ignoring a wide gap in the hedge halfway along to keep walking in the direction of the pylon line. The first view of the square tower of East Claydon church can be seen on the skyline. Cross the brook and go round the right corner of the field, then left along the wide grassy track with the hedge on the right (NW, 300°). Do not go through the wide metal gate near the brook. Continue on the left side of the hedge under the pylon line aiming for the church tower at **East Claydon**. At the end of the field continue on the bridleway between a fence on the left and a hedge on the right. The bridleway follows the right side of the hedgerow, ascending (NW) to join the lane leading towards the village.

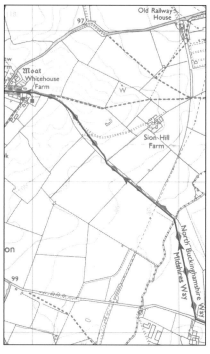

The first house we pass is Whitehouse Farm, an Elizabethan manor house, with a 17th-century porch, ancient door and a remarkable listed 18th-century garden wall, built of chequered brick with a moulded plinth at its base.

East Claydon (Old English – Clayey hill)
St Mary's Church is situated on the top of Sion Hill with the old London road passing on its north side. The earliest part of the church is from the 13th century. The organ has an interesting history in that it was originally built in 1665 for a church in Old Hackney in London. It was reputedly played by Handel. The chancel roof is a wooden hammerbeam roof while the nave has a 17th-century wagon-headed ceiling.
The main occupation in Victorian times was dairy farming, and until at least the 1860s the women and children made pillow lace. In the village are some remarkable cottages, for example, on the corner of the road to Botolph Claydon is an L-shaped timber-framed house of about 1600, with brick facing. The upper storey is jettied, the upper storey overhanging the lower. This was done partly for prestige, but also to increase the upper floor area.

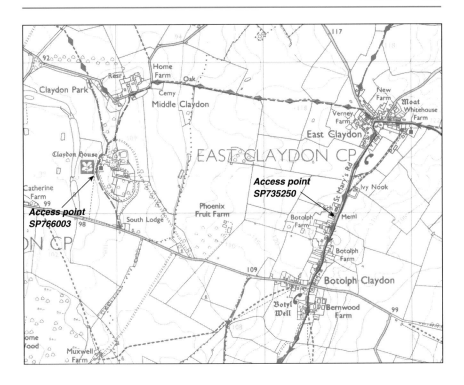

Optional diversion

Optional diversion to Middle Claydon and Claydon House where lunch is available. This is a 2.7 mile diversion (in total) across country as the roadway from Botolph Claydon is dangerous with no pavement or verges. To take this diversion from East Claydon, turn right on the road signed 'Padbury' to branch left after only 200 yards onto a footpath (W). Follow the hedgerow first on the right, then on the left and across the third field to join the right side of a hedge, still continuing west. At the wood on the left, continue along the hedgerow to arrive at the right side of the cemetery at Middle Claydon. Turn left on the road and past Home Farm on the right to turn left (S) across the field to walk beside a fence through the park pale to arrive in the gardens of Claydon House. The ticket office and restaurant are in the buildings beyond. At the end of the visit, retrace your steps using the same route back to East Claydon.

Claydon House (SP720254)
This is an eighteenth-century mansion set among water meadows and the family seat of the Verneys. Florence Nightingale's sister married into the Verney family so Florence was a frequent visitor, and her bedroom is preserved. The interior is a rich mixture of Palladian and rococo decoration.

National Trust. Open March–Nov, 11–5, not Thursdays and Fridays. Café and toilets. Tel: 01296 730349. www.nationaltrust.org.uk/claydon

'The Mushroom'

From East Claydon church turn left (W) to follow the street turning left again on the road signposted Botolph Claydon. There are jettied houses to the right and several gable-ended houses. Houses were often built with the windowless end towards the road for greater security. Pass a bus stop (service 16/17) then follow an enclosed tarmac footpath to the left of St Mary's Road. At the end of the enclosed part is 'The Mushroom', a circular seat with a thatched roof around the trunk of an old oak tree, built in 1912 by local artisans.

Continue SW past the village hall with its Mushroom Club, Old School House (1844) and clock tower dedicated to Sir Edward Verney in thanks for the gift of the village hall and school.

Access Point: Botolph Claydon, St Mary's Road. 4.6 miles (or 7.2 miles if diverting to Claydon House). SP735250.

Continue south to enter the village **Botolph Claydon** passing a fine Georgian house on the right and the dew pond of Botolph Farmhouse (B&B) to the left. At the road junction go ahead into a lane (S) taking great care in crossing the sharp bend.

Pass by the black-and-white timbered house with its protruding semi-circular bread oven in the wall to go through the yard of Bernwood Farm.

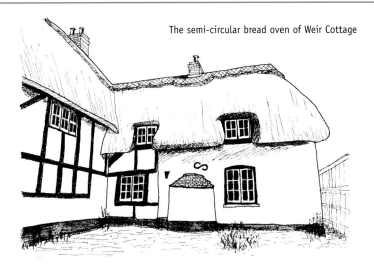

The semi-circular bread oven of Weir Cottage

Botolph Claydon

Botolph comes from the Old English word botl meaning 'house or building'. Botyl Well is supposedly dedicated to St Botwulf, an East Anglian Abbot who died c.680. However, this is unlikely, since there is no reason for St Botwulf to come this far west from his home base in Lincolnshire! Ancient holy wells were often dedicated to saints, but this was mainly to erase the possibility of pagan associations.

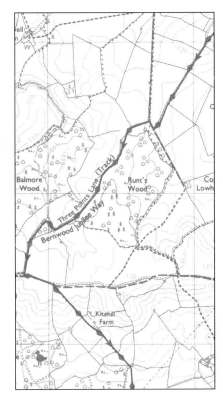

At the gate bear right (SW, 212°) across the field past the windsock to the hedgerow on the right side. At the next field boundary, continue along the left side of the hedgerow towards Runt's Wood, a surviving fragment of the ancient royal hunting forest of Bernwood.

At the wood turn right for 50 yards to then turn left (SW) along Three Points Lane, entering the wood at a noticeboard which describes the antiquity and rich biodiversity of this wood. Many of the species indicative of ancient woodland are present, such as pignut which flowers May–June. Continue along this well-marked track for ½ mile. At the point of the wood, where the path meets the field edge, bear right to follow the bridleway, then 400 yards further on is a wide metal gate. Turn left here onto a bridleway which is also part of the Bernwood Jubilee Way, a 61-mile route within the boundary of the ancient royal forest. After only 200 yards turn right over a stile, before the first field boundary. Go left around the field corner to descend the slope for 50 yards. Go left over a footbridge and a stile in the hedge. Here, bear slightly right (SE, 130°) aiming for the line of trees on the top of Grange Hill (*see map on p.139*) and towards the large complex of grey buildings left (N) of Grange Farm. Descend over the brow of the hill to go through a metal gate joining a footpath beside the ruins of Kitehill Farm. Continue downhill (SE) through the gap in a hedge, along the hedge boundary and over a double stile and footbridge to cross the horses' field. These horse paddocks are often squelchy as this is the site of springs. At the corner of Finemere Wood go through the

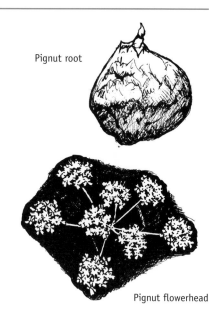

Pignut root

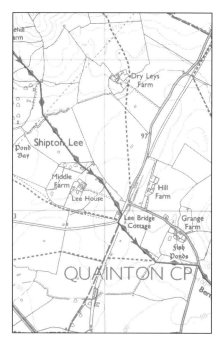

Pignut flowerhead

fence to bear slightly right (S, 178°) keeping left of the pylon, cross the field to go over the footbridge and stiles. Here, bear slightly left (SE, 140°) to cross the ancient meadow of Shipton Lee with its remains of ridge and furrow ploughing, aiming for the left side of a small wood on the far side. At the stile, continue to follow the Bernwood Jubilee Way by bearing left through the wood. Cross the next field, with Middle Farm to your right, passing a pond in the middle of the field, through another small wood, to turn left onto a track that leads to the road at Lee Bridge Cottage. Turn right for 50 yards to then turn left over a stile beside two metal gates. Take the footpath left (SE) across the dismantled railway line then uphill bearing slightly right (SE, 143°) to a wooden kissing gate. Go through this, to turn left along the field edge to a footbridge 30 yards to the right of the corner of the field. On entering the next field, there is a noticeboard explaining the significance of the medieval fish ponds (or stew ponds) of Grange Farm.

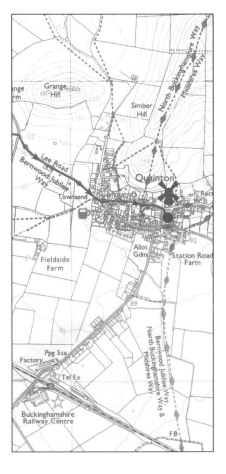

Stew Ponds
The notice board describes how only those of high status and religious institutions were allowed to have fish ('stew') ponds. Grange Farm was the home of the prestigious Dormer family (*see Ascott Park on the Great Haseley walk, p.87*).
The term 'stew' refers to a holding tank close to the kitchen where fish could be kept prior to being put into a 'stewing pot'.
People could not eat meat on Wednesdays, Fridays and Saturdays, during Lent, and on all main feast days. These days were known as 'Fish Days'.

(*Source* www.buckscc.gov.uk)

Follow the waymark (E) past an ancient wooden threshing machine to leave the field via a stile 15 yards right of the metal gate. At the road bear right along Lee Road signed 'Quainton 1'. Enter the village, bearing left at Towns End Farm on the right, to walk along Upper Street. There is a good example of thatched 'eyebrows' at The Boot cottage on the left (*see Mapledurham walk, p.108*). Pass Baker's Cottage to **Quainton** village green.

Buckinghamshire Railway Centre

If you wish to have tea in an historic railway buffet at the end of the walk, then this working steam locomotive centre is well worth a visit, particularly to Oxford residents, as the original Oxford Rewley Road Victorian cast iron station was moved here. The centre is 0.9 miles south of Quainton.

Tel: 01296 655720. www.bucksrailcentre.org

Rewley Road Station

Turville

Start and finish point SU777913

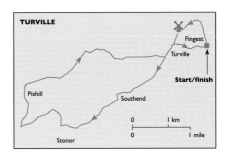

An energetic walk up and down the dry valleys of the Chiltern Hills and media country! We pass sites of popular interest such as the windmill featured in Chitty Chitty Bang Bang *and the church where* The Vicar of Dibley *was filmed. We walk beside the grand house of Stonor Park with its herd of fallow deer, and see two John Piper church windows. We finish at Fingest which was used for filming* Midsomer Murders *and George Clooney's* The Monuments Men.

Distance: 9.3 miles (14.5 km).

Maps: Explorer 171 – Chiltern Hills West.
Landranger 175 – Reading & Windsor, Henley-on-Thames & Bracknell.

Transport: Bus service now discontinued.

Taxis: Henley • Chiltern Cars. Tel: 01491 578899/414151.
bookings@chilterncars.com
• County Cars. Tel: 01491 579696.

Car Parking: Chequers Lane, next to Fingest Church. SU777913 (RG9 6QD).

Accommodation/Public Houses/Refreshments:
Turville • The Bull & Butcher. Tel: 01491 638283.
www.thebullandbutcher.com
Pishill • Crown Inn, B&B. 200 yards from the route (SU725900).
Tel: 01491 638364. www.thecrowninnpishill.co.uk
Fingest • The Chequers Inn. Tel: 01491 638335.
www.chequersfingest.com

141

Fingest

The most striking building in Fingest is the church which is Norman, with the most remarkable feature being the tall tower. It is a rare example of a turriform church, that is, a church which originally only had a tower with no nave. There are only a few others of this plan in England, one being at Broughton in Lincolnshire, and the other in Barton-on-Humber. The other very unusual feature is the twin saddleback roof.

The other buildings in the village built of the local flint and brick are the Old Rectory, a 17th century house, with its gable end facing the road. It has a small lych gate and faces the pub. This building was used for filming *Midsomer Murders*, and the Chequers Inn was disguised as an antique shop and used in the same series. The origin of the name 'Chequers' comes from a local 13th century exchequer clerk who served in the royal branch of government that collected taxes – likewise 'Chequers', the Prime Minister's country retreat near Ellesborough, a few miles away. The inn is decorated with a chequer-brick front with vitrified headers.

Fingest Church in the floods of February 2014

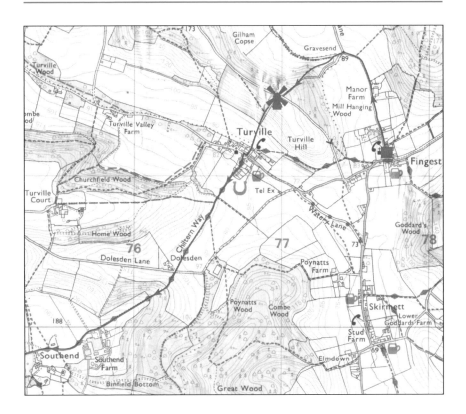

With your back to the church gate, turn left (N) along Chequers Lane, look out on the left for an iron-railed enclosure beside the large wooden gates of Fingest Manor. This was the parish pound where stray animals were deposited until their owners came to reclaim them.

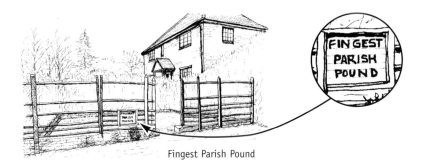

Fingest Parish Pound

Walk out of the village for nearly ½ mile, passing the huge barns of Manor Farm, the venue of the Fingest Great Barn Opera, on the right. Ignore a footpath on the right to arrive at Gravesend 100 yards after Manor Farm. Go beside the double metal gates, bear left, ignoring the yellow footpath sign to the left and the bridleway sign to the right. Instead go straight ahead, over a small stile by a gate, and continue uphill in the open meadow (SW, 223°).

This meadow has a chalkland flora and in August we found marjoram, basil, toadflax and mullein in flower.

When the footpath enters the wood, follow it uphill to the right of a wire/wooden fence (SW) to a road. Beware of the fast traffic as you cross the road. Dogleg right and left over the stile beside the mill.

Cobstone Windmill (SU769915)

Cobstone windmill in the parish of Ibstone is sometimes known locally as Turville windmill. Pevsner describes it as a smock mill (*see Lacey Green walk, p.93*) of about 1830 which replaced an earlier mill. This mill has three storeys, twelve sides rather than the usual six or eight sides, and a brick ground floor. It is weatherboarded above, with an ogee lead roof, has four sails and a fan tail. It featured in the film *Chitty Chitty Bang Bang*. The mill was converted to a house in about 1975, is in private ownership, and not open to the public.

For information see: www.britishlistedbuildings.co.uk

Descend the very steep hill, keeping by the large hedgerow on the left. It may be easier to zig-zag down as mountaineers do!

This rough pasture is rich in chalkland flowers and butterflies in summer. It forms part of the Wormsley Estate which is renowned for promoting biodiversity. It was here that red kites were first reintroduced into England.

Below is the village of **Turville**. It is worth turning around to get a good view of the windmill from the base of the hill.

Turville
Turville consists of mainly timber-framed and brick-and-flint houses, since flint was the main source of building material. The Bull and Butcher pub to the left is striking with its huge central chimney stack. To the right is the medieval St Mary's Church, also built of knapped flint. It has a beautiful John Piper window, made by Patrick Reyntiens, of a white hand with a lily against a deep blue background commemorating the closure of St Saviour's church, Turville Heath which we pass later in the walk. In recent times it has become popular with tourists as it was in this church that the TV series *The Vicar of Dibley* was filmed.

John Piper window, Turville Church

On meeting the village street, cross it, bearing right beside the small village green to enter a narrow lane beside a school notice. We join The Chiltern Way, passing 'Sleepy Cottage' on the right (SW) to follow a green lane with hazel coppicing on either side. Go through a gate into the open land.

The field to the left is part of the Bosmore Park Estate and is organically-managed land with wildlife conservation and biodiversity in mind. In the wide field margins to the left we saw the blue flowers of chicory and 'charms' (flocks) of goldfinches feeding on the thistle seeds. Red kites were wheeling overhead.

At the farm at **Dolesden**, take great care of fast cyclists and cars before crossing the road, go through the gate to climb a steeper slope through the woods and on to an asphalt track. On reaching a junction with another asphalt track, bear left to pass the buildings at Southend Farm to arrive in the small hamlet around the village green. **Southend** is a reference to the ancient boundaries of woodland in a similar way to the village name of Northend. The house by the road called 'Drovers' was formerly the pub, since the ironwork of the pub sign still remains on the left side of the building.

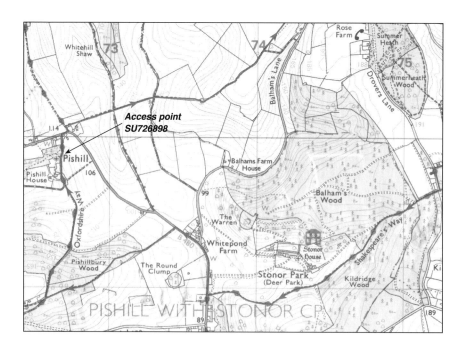

At the road turn left, then after 150 yards, turn right (SW) beside some cottages with decorative brickwork. We have now joined the Seven Shires Way, the Shakespeare Way, and the Macmillan Way. Enter the woods of Stonor Park with a field on the right. Where a track crosses our path 200 yards after the cottages is the county boundary of Buckinghamshire and Oxfordshire. Keep descending on the path, through the larch and silver birch woods with large rhododendron, bracken and foxgloves which all indicate that we are on acid soil. Go through a gate to enter the deer park to follow the path along the side of the valley in which Stonor House is sited.

The valley has some ancient oak trees and tall poplar trees which were heavy with mistletoe when we walked through in December. Thrushes and fieldfares were feeding on the berries of these trees.

Leave the park via a kissing gate by the road in the valley bottom.

Stonor House and Park
This name originates from the Old English *stanora* meaning 'at the stones', referring to the huge sarsen stones that were here in the 9th century. The ring of stones near the house is of recently gathered sarsens and is a modern folly. The estate has belonged to the Stonor family since the 12th century, and their private

letters still survive. 'The Stonor Correspondence 1290–1483' ranges from love letters to household accounts, giving a wealth of information about a gentry family, their servants and friends during the time of the Wars of the Roses. The family is Catholic and suffered in the 16th century since they were recusants (people who refused to attend Anglican services). The medieval house has a 14th century chapel to the right, priest holes, secret passages and an Elizabethan brick façade.

House open: Sun & BH Mons (April–Sept), also Weds & Thurs (June, July & Aug) 1.30–5.30. Tea room, chapel & gardens: open at 12. Admission charges.
Tel: 01491 638587. www.stonor.com

Cross the road to turn right (N) along a path beside the road for 300 yards, with views of the deer park on the right. Go past the 'Ahead Only' sign and beside the cricket pitch and into the field on the far side. Where the path bears right to the road, it is possible to continue along beside the hedgerow to avoid the road by White Pond Farm. Go towards a long ancient hedgerow which ascends the hill. At the hedgerow, turn left into an enclosed green lane to climb the hill (SW) through Pishillbury Wood.

Management of Pishillbury Wood

This is a wood of mixed beech trees and hazel coppicing with male ferns and a woodland pond. Coppicing (or cutting down) is a traditional practice to produce hazel sticks for fencing and charcoal making. Interspersed between the hazel are the large maiden or standard beech trees (*see Combe walk, p.62*), which were used for building. Woodland management is cyclical, having trees at all stages of growth. Pollarded trees are cut off at head height (poll) so that the new shoots are out of reach for cattle and deer. In August we saw the remarkable pale yellow-coloured fungus known as sulphur polypore or 'chicken of the woods' (*Laetiporus sulphureus*).

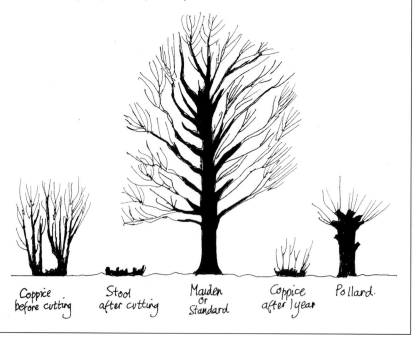

Coppice before cutting · Stool after cutting · Maiden or Standard · Coppice after 1 year · Pollard.

Walk for ½ mile in the wood to the far boundary. Here turn sharp right (NE) to join the Oxfordshire Way. Follow the footpath downhill, crossing a track that leads to Doyley Wood, and up and down on the right side of a field, alongside an old hedgerow, to go through a gate in the field corner. Turn right and down the lane passing the large vicarage to the small, flint and stone, rebuilt Norman church at **Pishill** (Old English – Peose hyll 'pea hill').

The church has an unusual T-shaped nave, Victorian glass and another John Piper stained glass window. This window portrays St Paul's symbols, the sword and the gospel. The gospel is held by two hands in front of the sword, signifying that the pen is mightier than the sword. There is also another modern window in the second nave, depicting the 16th century hymn 'God be in my head...'

Access Point: Pishill Church car park 5.5 miles. Pub, B&B. SU726898.

Continue down the narrow lane to the road. The pub is 200 yards (W) to the left.

From the church lane turn right (E) along the road to Pishill Farmhouse and turn left at a sharp bend. Walk for only 30 yards on the Oxfordshire Way, to turn right over an obscure stile to follow the footpath (NE) beside the farmhouse garden. Continue on this path uphill to cross a gravel bridleway and continue on in the same direction (NE) downhill to descend the slope. This is beside a newly planted lime avenue celebrating 75 years of farming by the Stracey family at White Pond Farm. Go through an old hedgerow, across a second bridleway to ascend the slope opposite across the open field. In the small wood near the top of the slope is a seat in memory of 'Pop' Stracey.

Glaciated valleys in the Chilterns
Although the ice sheets did not reach this part of England, the landscape was sculpted into its present form by powerful erosional forces due to the climatic extremes. Huge volumes of melt water swelled the rivers giving them power to transport vast quantities of rock waste which was deposited as boulder clay. This Northern Drift, as the deposits are known, is composed of flint and clay. The deeper clay supports the growth of trees such as the beech woods on the Chilterns. The mass of chalk fragments, with or without flints is called Combe Rock and forms the valley floors of Fingest and Turville.
(Philip Powell, *The Geology of Oxfordshire*, 2005).

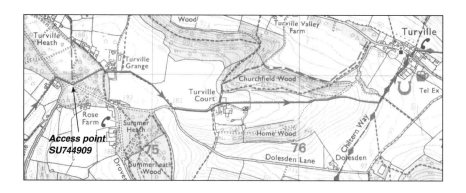

Follow the footpath on the right of the ancient, multi-specied hedgerow with huge field maple, beech, ash and hawthorn trees. Be careful not to miss an iron kissing gate on the left. Go through it and across the parkland of the large house, Turville Park. Cross the field (NE) over a stile towards the house and go through two kissing gates in the direction of a row of brick cottages. Keep a large beech tree to the right and curve left beside a lawn of a converted Gothic style church, St Saviour's, where the bellcote still remains and a cross in the brickwork is visible (*see John Piper window in Turville Church, p.145*). Go beside the house gates to enter an enclosed footpath.

Access Point: Turville Heath, near the bus shelter and public bridleway sign. 7 miles. Car parking along the lime avenue. SU744909.

At the road, turn right, then left with the bus shelter to the left, beside the small triangular green, along the minor road marked 'Turville and Fingest', to then turn left on a tarmac drive (NE) opposite the road sign marked 'Stonor and Henley' towards a large house, Turville Grange, at its end.

Turville Grange
Turville Grange is an early 18th century house of vitreous and red brick with denticulated (like a row of teeth) decoration below the gutters and an elegant shell porch style. The garden wall is also decorated with pineapple finials. The wrought-iron gates were given by Queen Alexandra, wife of Edward VII, who was a frequent visitor of the former owner, the Marquis d'Hautpoul.

Turn right at the Grange to turn left (E) through a large gate on the far right of the house, past an ancient pump, to go through another gate ahead (NB do not turn left on a footpath leading north). Follow the hedge on the right for 100 yards to turn right over a double stile in the hedge. On the other side, turn left to walk with the hedge on your left for 100 yards (or $2/_3$ of the hedge length) to then bear diagonally left across the field (SE, 140°) to follow a wire fence along its right side. There is a small gate in the far left corner of the field where there is an option to either turn left here to follow a permissive path between trees parallel to the road, or if this is overgrown, descend onto the road, taking care of the traffic, to turn left along the road leading to Turville Court. At the house follow the path around the drive to go through a small gate onto a track. Do not turn left into the wood, but go through a large gate onto a bridleway (E). Descend the hill gradually while walking parallel to the beech hanger, Churchfield Wood. At a small gate beside a larger one, keep left alongside the wood for 150 yards to a bench. Here bear right (E, 90°) down the open field to a double wooden gate at the field bottom. Turn left, rejoining the same path that we used earlier. Follow the green lane into **Turville** to bear right beside the village green to follow a footpath opposite towards the windmill for 100 yards. Go through the first gate, then turn immediately right through another gate on the Chiltern Way.

We are back on the chalk grassland with the rich mix of wildflowers, and here we saw the blue clustered bellflower and wild thyme growing. A small group of fallow deer were feeding on the ridge above us.

Cross the field (E) following the contours of this dry valley around Turville Hill (SE) in an enclosed green lane. Cross a minor road and continue on the path in the wood for 100 yards. Here turn right (E) onto a narrow footpath between a wattle fence on the left and a flint wall on the right, towards the village of **Fingest**. At the road turn left past the church and pub to turn left (N) into Chequers Lane.

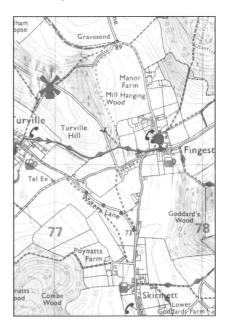

Mill Mechanics

Both windmills and watermills use the power from the rotating motion of the sails or water wheels via a system of gearwheels to turn the millstones that grind the grain. The stones themselves, very often in pairs, were of various origins. The best came from continental quarries, especially from the Rhineland. However, they were heavy and transport was costly, so mill owners began to rely on home-produced Millstone Grit from the Pennine quarries in Derbyshire. Another popular stone was French Burr: blocks of quartz quarried near Paris, were set like giant jigsaws in cement and plaster of Paris and bound together with iron hoops. The miller needed to dress the stone carefully to produce a smooth working surface. These surfaces were covered by a system of grooves or 'furrows', using a steel drill or cutting tool. This furrowed surface performed the central process of grinding. The flour or meal was expelled to the outside of the stone along the furrows.

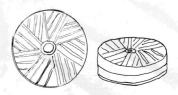

Millstones

In Britain, oak was favoured for the mechanism and shaft which drove the mill. Cogs, on the other hand, the small peg-like pieces attached to the various wheels, were made of applewood, or other hard woods such as hornbeam or beech. For the floats of water wheels, elm was used because of its resistance to rot in water. Iron might be used sparingly for bearings but in the 19th century large-scale production made it possible to cast the pit wheel and the wallower (a small gear driven by the pit wheel) as well as the fastenings and the tie-rods. The great spur wheels, however, continued to be made of timber.

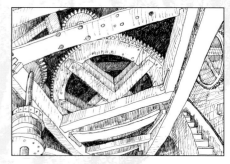

Great Spur Wheel

Tysoe

Start and finish point SP339442

We leave from the Warwickshire village of Middle Tysoe, to climb up to Tysoe windmill which overlooks the grand Tudor manor house of Compton Wynyates. This is a hilly walk in ironstone country, where the houses are built of ginger-coloured stone. We descend back to Upper and Middle Tysoe.

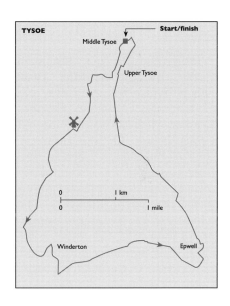

Distance: 9.1 miles (14.6 km).

Maps: Explorer 206 – Edge Hill & Fenny Compton.
Landranger 151 – Stratford-upon-Avon & surrounding area.

Transport: Buses   • Stagecoach Midland Red 50A. Stratford–Banbury.
                          • Johnson's 270. Stratford–Banbury.

Taxis: Banbury   • Banbury Taxis Ltd. Tel: 01295 272727.
                          • Banbury Cars. Tel: 01295 233689.

Car Parking: Near the Peacock Inn and Tysoe Village Stores, Middle Tysoe. SP339442
(CV35 0SE).

Accommodation/Public Houses/Refreshments:

Epwell • The Chandler's Arms. Tel: 01295 780747.

Middle Tysoe • The Peacock Inn. Tel: 01295 680338.

• The Tysoe Village Stores and Tearoom.
Tel: 01295 688333. tysoevillagestores@googlemail.com

Oxhill • Nolands Farm B&B. 1.5 miles from Middle Tysoe
(SP312470). Tel: 01926 640309. www.nolandsfarm.co.uk

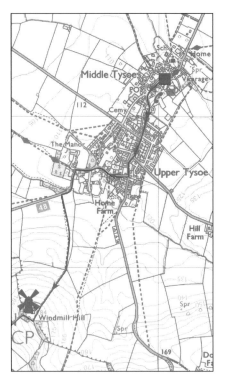

From the Peacock Inn walk south through **Middle Tysoe** village, which has good examples of thatched ironstone cottages. Keep on Main Street (SW) through **Upper Tysoe**. On the right (W) edge of the village green in Back Lane is one of the several water sources that have biblical quotes in the plaques on the walls. Take great care of the traffic coming round the bends. Continue on this main road, turning right, towards the outside of the village passing Garden Cottage on the right with its fine brick walls and organic garden (there are often fruit and vegetables for sale here). On reaching a small wood on the right, there is a waymark on the left. Go through a small gate to start climbing the hill (S, 19°) on the footpath gradually converging with the hedgerow. Continue up on the right of the hedge to the windmill.

From the windmill continue walking first south to a metal kissing gate, where there is a good view of Compton Wynyates below. Turn immediately right beside the stone wall, to turn left steeply downhill (SW) with views of the original watermill leat on the SE side of the small wood NW of Compton Wynyates.

Tysoe Windmill

The windmill is an early 18th-century stone tower mill with a restored metal-roofed cap. The sails consist of stocks (spars) only, though inside the wooden mill machinery still exists. The view from the mill includes the Vale of the Red Horse, stretching north from the base of Edge Hill, with views as far as Gaydon, with the white roofs of the Aston Martin headquarters and Coventry beyond, and to the west across the Cotswolds to the Malvern Hills.

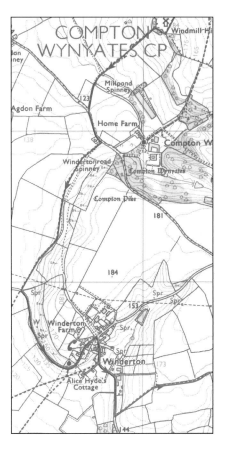

At the bottom of the hill, go straight ahead over a stile, beside a large metal gate along the track, to turn left at the road for 250 yards, then right over a stile after some cottages.

Go along the path (S, 210°) where there is a line of springs at the bottom of the slope where the water meets the impervious clay and comes to the surface at the base of the layer of the ironstone that forms these hills.

There were gorse bushes in flower when we walked in April and we saw buzzards overhead.

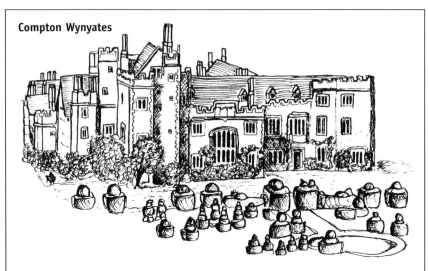

Compton Wynyates

The grand Tudor brick-built house of Compton Wynyates lies in a hollow of
several small hills. The origin of 'Wynyates' is 'windy' and the house was known
in the past as 'Compton-in-the-Hole', a reference to the village which was
destroyed to create the spacious park around Sir William Compton's new home.
Although it is now closed to the public, in winter it is possible to see the
castellated and turreted house built around a central courtyard. It was formerly
moated. William Compton was a ward of the Crown during his childhood and
became a page to Prince Henry, subsequently King Henry VIII. He and the King
became good friends and Henry stayed many times in a bedroom that still
retains the stained glass window showing his and Catherine of Aragon's coats of
arms. Several other monarchs stayed here including Elizabeth I, James I and
Charles I and there is a bedroom decorated with their monograms. The Compton
family, the current Marquesses of Northampton, still live in the house.

At the road do not take the footpath opposite but turn left (SE) along
the road towards **Winderton** taking care of the traffic. Enter the village
to turn sharp right down the road (S) to pass Alice Hyde's Cottage
(marked only on the map). Go on south to leave the village, but at the
first footpath by a hedge on the left take path number 54a to start climbing again (NE) to walk along the left side (S) of a hedge, then across three
fields uphill to join a bridle track at a stile near the top of the hill. Follow
the bridle track past the cottage on the right and through a wood to join

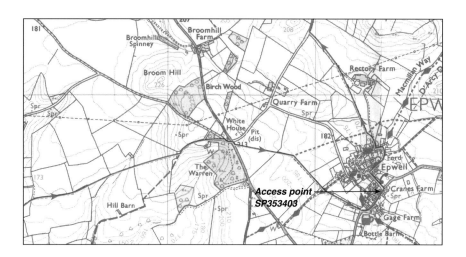

a road. Turn right here to a crossroads at the White House (marked only on the map). At the junction cross over the road signposted 'Sibford and Banbury', turn right to immediately go through a gate on the left (SE) and downhill across a field descending to the village of **Epwell**. At the end of a hedge, take the right (SE) path along the right side of a hedge, crossing the Macmillan Way to continue on beside the hedge to arrive at the back of The Chandler's Arms pub. (A chandler was someone who made candles.)

Access Point: The Chandler's Arms pub, 6 miles. Bus (once a day only). SP353403.

From the Chandler's Arms turn left to walk past the well (100 yards NE of the pub). The house beside the well has a catslide roof (*see p.158*).

Turn left at the sign 'Epwell Village. No Through Lorries' and proceed to The Square. Here we meet the route of *The Seven Shires Way* a 234 mile walk (created by the author) following close to the Oxfordshire county boundary. At the churchyard corner go along Back Lane (NW) which curves right. After 200 yards, turn left (N) along the lane that is the *second* waymarked footpath, immediately beyond Rose Cottage and before Rectory Cottage. At a stile in the first field, bear left (N, 320°) of the farm track, to cross the field to a stile and footbridge over a small brook to the left of the track. From the brook bear diagonally left (NW, 338°) along the right side of an ancient hedge full of crab apple trees.

Epwell, catslide roof
Many of the village houses are built of a ginger-coloured (iron impregnated) shelly sandstone. Some are thatched and the steep pitch of other roofs betray the fact that they had previously been thatched. The roofs had to be steeply pitched for the rain to fall off quickly. The house beside the well is a good example of a catslide roof: a long, gently-sloping roof built to cover an out-building; it often nearly reaches the ground so that a cat could slide down it, though that is not its principal purpose!

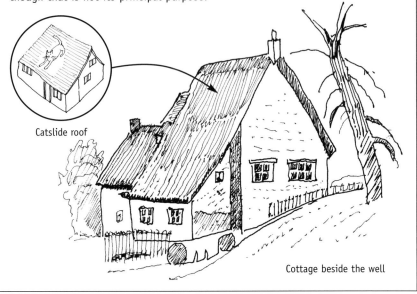

Catslide roof

Cottage beside the well

Yarn Hill, a flat-topped hill covered with gorse and bracken, can be seen to the east. Keep to the same direction as the first part of the hedge line to where it bears left after a short distance and cross the field passing left (W) of Rectory Farm. Keep left of a pylon to reach a wooden gate and onto a farm track. Turn left. There are some good examples of ridge and furrow in the field on the left. Walk along this track (NW) to the road in front of Orchard Hill. Turn right (N) at the road and after 180 yards turn left (NW) onto a farm track to Downs Farm. At the end of the first field, bear right (NW, 328°) to a small wooden gate and footbridge in the corner of a field in the county boundary hedgeline. This hedge is wide and twisting compared to the straight narrow enclosure hedge that we have just passed through.

Goldfinch

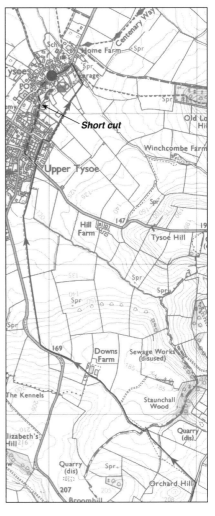

The county boundary also has a ditch and a much richer plant life that attracts more diverse species of birds. We saw goldfinches feeding on the thistle seed beside the boundary.

Go through a wooden gate and cross the stream into **Warwickshire**, then turn left with the stream on the left. *Do not* go through the metal gate across the ditch, instead turn right, (NW) up hill on the right-hand side of a hedge along the cart track to Downs Farm. Go through the yard and down the track to the road. Turn right and walk down the road for 150 yards to where a footbridge and a kissing gate cross the hedgerow on the right side of the road. In the field, walk half-left down it (N, 354°) and keep your eye on the red pantiles of Rose Farm in Upper Tysoe below, once these becomes visible over the brow of the hill. Tysoe windmill can be seen again to the left. Aim for the stile to the left of the lone ash tree in the first hedgerow, then down the next field to cross the bridge over the brook in front of Home Farm. Walk behind the houses of Upper Tysoe keeping

Rose Farm to the left. Continue through a kissing gate in the corner to walk (N) along a narrow path between a field and an orchard. Go over a stile onto a path behind the house gardens and beside allotments, and through a wooden gate onto a road in **Middle Tysoe**.

Short Cut
For a short cut, turn left here to the main village street then right (N) back to the Peacock Inn.

To see remarkable evidence of medieval ridge and furrow ploughing, walk (N) behind the village of Middle Tysoe. To do this, dogleg left and right, to walk (N) along Middleton Close. Keep straight to the end, aiming for the green-painted garages. Turn right along Welshman Place (not along Avon Way), then go left before the wall of a white-painted garage, and continue on the path along the left-hand edge of a football pitch. Go through a stile to see ridge and furrow fields on the right side of the path (E). For more information on ridge and furrow see Brill walk, p.34.

To continue the route, keep north, then turn left through a metal gate into a small paddock, then right to keep to the left-hand edge of a small wood. Cross over a stile in the right-hand corner and cross another field in the direction of a small wrought-iron gate. Do not go through the gate, but turn sharp left and through a steel gate onto a narrow path. At the second iron gate turn right between the gardens, keeping the brick garden wall to the right. Peacock Lane is at the end of this path. Turn left into the lane to join the main street by a former fountain with its biblical quotes near the church.

The church is a rare, Grade 1 listed building, dating back to the eleventh century at least. There is an octagonal Perpendicular font and a beautiful clerestory (part of the church wall above the aisle roof which has a series of windows). Of interest too, is a stone effigy of William Clarke in Elizabethan dress. It shows his costume well, with its cap, ruff, buttoned doublet and hose.

Middle Tysoe

For those with geological interests, in the walls of the building just before the Peacock Inn, on the right (W), opposite L. J. Carter's (a family butcher), there are streaks of iron ore as well as fossilised shells in the ironstone. Incidentally, the house next door to the butcher on the left is called Scrag End!

'Scrag End' cottage

Sails

Just as the paddles of a water wheel capture the force of the water, sails on a windmill harness the force of the moving air. The sails need to twist the force of the wind to make the shaft inside rotate. By putting sailcloth on the lattice framework of the sails, a flat surface is created: these were known as common sails and, just as a sailor would do, the miller could adjust the amount of cloth according to the amount of wind available and power needed.

Sailcloth

The disadvantage of this design was that every time the sails needed adjusting, the mill had to be stopped with the consequent loss of income. The patent sail was invented by William Cubitt in 1813, with sailcloth replaced by a mechanism of connected shutters which could be adjusted to the wind speed rather like the flaps of an aircraft wing (*see Wilton Windmill, p.196*).

The majority of windmills have four sails. The reason for this is by having an even number of sails the mill can operate with a damaged sail with its opposite removed without unbalancing. Since the sails could be manually turned to different positions, millers could send messages (and still do). The usual position of sails is the St Andrew's Cross, but could be changed to the St George's Cross position to send messages to the village, such as alerts for danger, for celebrations, or in respect on the death of a fellow miller.

In the Netherlands, a slight tilt of the sails before the main building signals joy, while a tilt after the building, mourning. All the windmills were in the mourning position in respect of the Dutch victims of the 2014 Malaysian Airlines Flight 17 shootdown.

St. Andrew's Cross

St. George's Cross

Wantage

Start and finish point SU398873

We start from the old market town of Wantage, passing King Alfred's statue and the working roller mill near the John Betjeman Millennium Park. From there we walk to the spring-line villages of Letcombe Regis and Letcombe Bassett to climb to the Ridgeway on the Berkshire Downs.

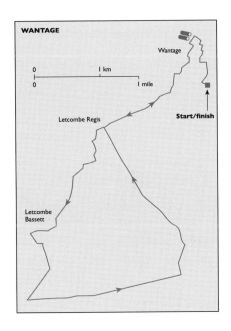

Distance: 8.7 miles (14 km).

Maps: Explorer 170 – Abingdon, Wantage & Vale of White Horse.
Landranger 174 – Newbury, Wantage & surrounding area.

Transport: Buses   • Oxford to Wantage, X30/31.
                        • Didcot to Wantage, X1/X32.
                        • Letcombe Regis to Wantage. Whites Thames Travel, 38/67/47.

Taxis: Wantage   • Secure Car Services. Tel: 07557 229227.
                        • Stuart's Taxis. Tel: 01235 770608.
                        • Supercab Taxis. Tel: 01235 770000.
                        • Webb's of Wantage. Tel: 01235 772000, mob. 07881 647777.

Car Parking: Manor Road Memorial Park, Manor Road. SU398873 (OX12 8DW). NB: This is on the left, just past the school and Comrades Club — easy to miss.

Accommodation/Public Houses/Refreshments:

Letcombe Regis	• Richmond Lodge shop and café. Tel: 01235 774789.
	• Greyhound Inn. Tel: 01235 771093. www.greyhoundinnletcomberegis.co.uk
The Ridgeway	• Court Hill Centre, B&B and suppers, café, toilets. Tel: 01235 760253. www.courthill.org.uk
Wantage	• The Bear Hotel. Tel: 01235 766366. www.thebearwantage.co.uk.
	• Vale and Downland Museum café, 9.30–4.00, Mon–Sat. Tel: 01235 771447.
	• Costa Coffee House at Arbery's, Market Square.
Wantage	• Tourist Information at Vale and Downland Museum, Church Street, Wantage. Tel: 01235 760176. www.wantage-museum.com

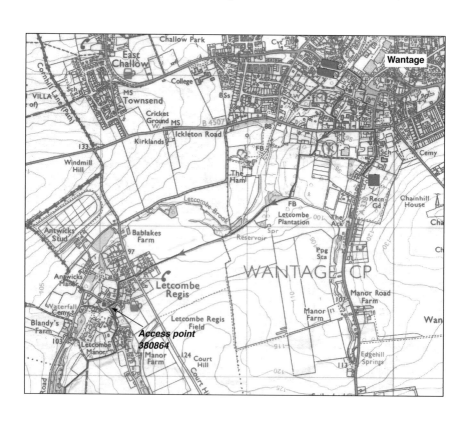

From the Manor Road car park turn right (N) along Newbury Street where there are terraces of decorated brick houses. There are ridge tiles, platbands and pargetting of the gables with an ornate iron porch at No. 53. On the right is the former St Mary's Girls School, now Gabriel House. At the traffic lights use the crossing, then turn left (W) into Portway where there is another brick terrace. After 50 yards, turn right (N) into the Civic Hall car park and continue through it, past the toilets on the far side, to meet Church Street where 100 yards to the left the Museum and Tourist Information Point are located. Cross Church Street to go through the Arbery Arcade. It is possible to enter the rear of Costa Coffee shop, previously Arbery's Drapers, where some of the original fittings have been preserved (see box).

Costa Coffee's Lamson Pneumatic Tube System
On the right of the counter is a long bendy copper pipe going up through the ceiling. This was a method of transferring change and receipts around the shop in capsules using compressed air. It is still possible to press the pedal which would have sent the capsule on its way. The assistants on the shop floor were able to send money to the cashier above, who could promptly send down change and a receipt. This was common from Victorian times and is still in use in some places. The House of Commons, for example, has a telephone and computer exchange system still employing this pneumatic tube system, and there was even one in NASA's original Mission Control Centre.

The whole 16th-century building is of historic interest; the original shop front from c.1890, frosted front doors and 'barley-sugar' twist columns remain. The upper windows are inscribed 'Corsets, Costumes, Millinery, Dressmaking & the Boot and Shoe Department'. Records show that in 1926 someone bought a brassiere for 2/9d (17½p)!

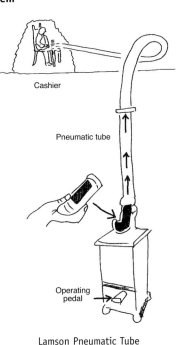

Cashier

Pneumatic tube

Operating pedal

Lamson Pneumatic Tube

In the square is the statue of King Alfred the Great.

Alfred the Great

King Alfred (849-901) was born at Wantage and was instrumental in defeating the Danes at Wilton in Wiltshire. He is buried at Hyde Abbey in Winchester. Alfred was remarkable in that he established a central system of government through burghs (now boroughs). He also founded schools to re-establish literacy after the ravages of the Viking invaders. He is the only English King to be called 'Great'. The story of him burning the cakes is probably folklore.

Turn left past the Bear Hotel with its cobbled courtyard near the main bus stop and continue in the same direction towards the King Alfred's Head pub, turn right to descend Alfred Street to cross Mill Street using the crossing. Go left downhill, passing some almshouses on a raised pavement on the left side. Continue down to the bottom of the hill where, on arriving at the small green by the Wharf, there is an information board about the history of the mill opposite and of the canal.

From the mill shop, turn right to go along a narrow path beside the old mill leat to the left of the current mill. The original waterwheel is now behind a timber fence. After only 100 yards there is a bridge at Betjeman Lane.

To the right is the Betjeman Millennium Park, a pleasant green space that was formerly allotments. A notice explains that Sir John Betjeman (1906–1984) and his wife Penelope lived in Wantage. He was the Poet Laureate from 1972 and has been described as the man 'who made words sing'. There is a circle of small standing stones, a folly mimicking a prehistoric stone circle.

Retrace your steps to the bridge, cross it, and go up Betjeman Lane where there is a chance to visit St Peter and St Paul's Church on the left. Turn right (SW) into Priory Road. Further along the road a blue plaque says that this was previously known as Tanners' Street since the cottages were occupied by the workers in the tanneries up to the end of the 18th century.

The brickwork on the cottages is decorative, with platbands and vitrified 'black headers'. Here the vitrified bricks have been used decoratively to produce a chequered effect. The end of the brick was dipped in glaze, but sometimes whole bricks are treated to make them impermeable and resistant to corrosion.

Wessex Flour Mill

The board explains that the original mill used the Letcombe Brook as its source of power. The former wharf at the terminus of the canal nearby made the transport of grain and flour easier. Next to it is the Wessex Mill, a roller mill built in 1910, which was originally an all-biscuit-flour mill. It now specialises in producing flour from local farms, listed on the bags of unusual flour mixes, which are sold in its shop, online and elsewhere. Shop open Monday–Friday, 8–5.

The mill offers free tours.
Tel: 01235 768991.
www.wessexmill.co.uk

Wessex Mill, shop window

Where Locks Lane enters from the right, there is a kink in Priory Road so dogleg left and right, first passing the buildings of King Alfred's School to the left and more cottages on the right which have delicate iron railings that survived the World War II policy to reclaim iron for the war effort. At the road, Portway, cross with great care to go between the stone pillars opposite into an enclosed footpath. Follow this path to turn right at a junction after a tile-hung cottage. Go around the side of a football pitch, along a path to go over a bridge of a tributary of the Letcombe Brook. The water beside the path is clear with mint growing in it.

Continue along an asphalt path with iron railings to the right. The clump of fir trees visible (SW) at the top of the Ridgeway are the Sparsholt Firs (SU341845). The outskirts of the village of **Letcombe Regis** are reached. At the crossroads go straight ahead towards the church and Letcombe Bassett. Walk along beside the wall passing The closed Greyhound Inn, with more black-glazed vitrified bricks, to the left.

Letcombe Regis and a young Maori Chieftain
The origin of the name comes from Ledecumbe – lede in the combe – meaning 'the brook in the valley'. There is an old legend, however, which says that the name stems from a battle in the area between the Saxons and the Danes when the enemy's blood flowed and the locals cried "Let it come! Let it come!" This story is unsubstantiated. The 'Regis' part comes from the fact that the manor was originally a royal one. King John had a hunting lodge here.

The 15th-century church of St Andrew has a 13th-century tower and 14th-century glass. Beside the path to the right is a tall obelisk, a memorial built in memory of a Maori chieftain, George King Hipango who sadly died of tuberculosis in 1871 at the age of 19 while he was staying at the vicarage training as a missionary.

To the left of the church is the entrance of Richmond Village Retirement Home with its circular thatched café and shop, open to the public.

Maori memorial, Letcombe Regis

It was from the Inn steps that the Riot Act was read in the 1900s, apparently for the last time in England, after the villagers had burnt an effigy of the unpopular owner of Antwicks Manor.

Follow the road round to a crossroads.

We admired the unusual end of the house on the corner (Yew Tree Cottage) dated 1707. It is built of a traditional mix of flint and sarsen stones with an external iron bracket securing the tie beam inside. Above is the opening for a sack hoist and below on the right is a filled-in window designed to dodge the window tax (see Brill walk, p.29).

Access point: Letcombe Regis Church 2.2 miles, bus, café. SU380864.

Take the road (S) marked 'Village and Downs Only' to pass the restored village pump to the right (water would have been very important in these spring-line villages) and on the left the Old Reading Room, now a cottage. Continue along South Street on the raised path to the sharp corner to the left at its end. Here turn right (SW) along the footpath to bear left (S).

Alternative route

At the sign of the Letcombe Valley Nature Reserve, it is possible to go through a small metal gate onto a permissive path to bear left down across a meadow towards the river. Go through another kissing gate and stay on the lower woodchip path ignoring the first path rising up to the left. Continue through the Nature Reserve to then climb a steep slope past a bench to go through a gate, turning right onto the footpath to Letcombe Bassett. Below the site of the bench is a thatched, black-and-white timbered house beside the brook where the 'Cresscombe Mill' mentioned in Thomas Hardy's *Jude the Obscure* was situated.

Jude the Obscure
Thomas Hardy took this landscape as the setting for his tragic novel about a working class stonemason's unsuccessful attempt to enter Oxford University. Jude imagined he could see the bright lights of Oxford from 'The Red Barn' on the Ridgeway. He was waylaid in his scholarly attempts by being seduced by Arabella, who was washing pigs' chitterlings in the Letcombe Brook.

Letcombe Valley Nature Reserve
This nature reserve, opened in 2010, borders the
Letcombe Brook which is one of the rare chalk
stream habitats. Water voles, bullheads (small
fish) and brook lampreys, a primitive form
of fish, all protected species, breed here.
Our route passes the reedbeds on the right
and in May, birdsong filled the wooded valley sides.

For more information see: www.bbowt.org.uk

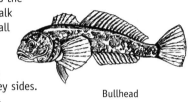

Bullhead

Follow the narrow path to meet the road on the edge of **Letcombe Bassett**, a village famed for its watercress as the old London street market cries of "Bassett Cress!" testify. The watercress beds can still be seen in the valley below to the right. On meeting the road, turn left uphill with race-horse stables to the left, and pass the road signposted 'To the Downs'. Keep right, towards Childrey, to arrive at Arabella's Cottage beside the stream, opposite the 'Yew Tree'.

Beyond Arabella's Cottage, the pool that is the source of the Letcombe Brook can be seen over the beech hedge below a house called 'Delamere'. Continue to Holborn Farmhouse on the right, with its wide elm planks, then double back left up the path in front of the houses beside Spanswick Farm to turn right at the left of the row of houses into an enclosed path. Go through the metal gate and on uphill into the open downland. At an isolated hand gate, turn left along a former hedge-line. Before reaching a waymark post in the field before the church, turn right to start climbing uphill on the right side of an avenue of ash trees.

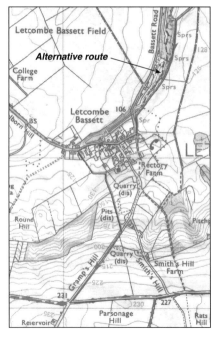

Arabella's Cottage, Letcombe Bassett

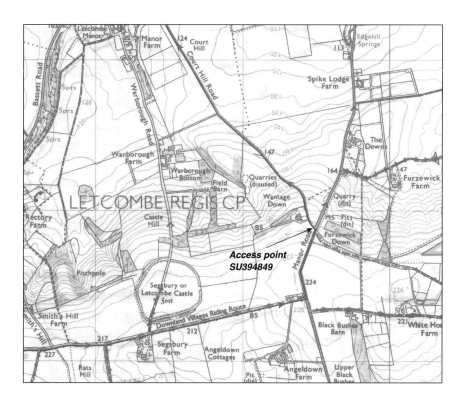

Should you wish to make the 200 yard diversion to St Michael's Church, it is well worth seeing the fine carving of the Norman chancel arch. In April the churchyard was a carpet of blue anemone blanda and yellow primroses.

Continue uphill through the next gate along the right side of the hedge from where there are wonderful views back across the Vale of White Horse.

This is where the glacial meltwater scoured the landscape and made huge bowl-like hollows such as the Devil's Punchbowl to the left.

Near the top, just past the corner where the edge of the field curves right, turn left to enter a narrow gap through the hedge, and turn right up the road (Gramp's Hill) to the Ridgeway. Here turn left to walk with views north towards Oxford and south towards the Berkshire Downs. Continue along the ancient route of the Ridgeway to arrive at a signpost 'Letcombe Regis 2.5 km/1.6 miles'.

Here is an opportunity to make a 100-yard diversion to see the ramparts of Segsbury Camp, an Iron Age hillfort. In April it was carpeted with yellow cowslips.

Retrace your steps to the Ridgeway to turn left (E) and past a cluster of houses on the site of The Red Barn (see Jude the Obscure box), to arrive at the main road. Turn left here and take great care to keep on the verges, the traffic can be very fast here. On the left (W) bank take a path hidden behind a hedgerow. From here there are good views down to Wantage. On meeting the road turn left to the Court Hill Centre. Further downhill is a milestone, in the verge on the A338, where Hardy writes that Jude carved his ambitions "THITHER ➤" pointing in the direction of Oxford.

Access point: The Court Hill Centre, 6.2 miles. Parking, café, accommodation. SU394849.

Court Hill Centre, The Ridgeway

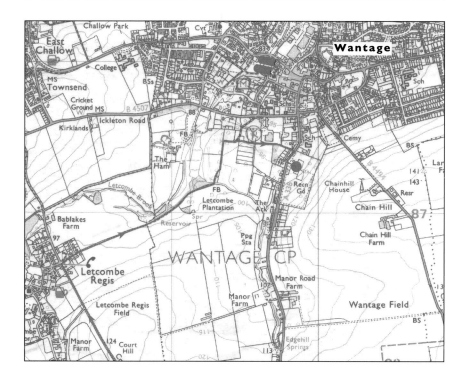

From the Centre, cross the road with care to descend the hill along a bridle track (NW) just right of the road. On nearing the village of Letcombe Regis follow the road down to turn right at the crossroads. Retrace your steps of the outward journey to Letcombe Brook and go around the left side of the football pitch. At the tile-hung house, turn right and follow the footpath (E) past a leisure centre along a green lane to meet the road opposite the metal gates of the Manor Road Park on the south side of Wantage. Cross the road into the Memorial Park recreation ground with its Victorian iron bandstand, drinking fountain and toilets and car park beyond.

Tide Mills

Britain's island status with its sea tides means that this force can also be harnessed, both on the coastline and on river estuaries. A few of these mills (beyond the geographical scope of this book) are in working order and open to the public. An example of this is Eling Tide Mill on Southampton Water dating from the 14th century. This working mill relies on the difference between low and high tides to provide the necessary head of water. A dam was built to create a storage area (mill pond) and at the other end is a sluice gate under the mill to let the water out. In practice about seven hours of milling (albeit dictated by tide times) could be achieved.

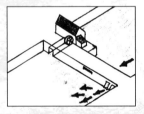

Tide Rising – The water comes in through the sea hatches to fill the tide pond

High Tide – The tide pond is full and the sluice is closed to maintain the head of water

Tide Falling – 1½ hours after high tide the sluice is opened and the mill runs until 2 hours before the next high tide

These illustrations have been taken from the Eling Tide Mill Guide

The Three Tide Mills on the River Lea in East London (said to be the largest tide mill in the world), Carew Castle in Pembrokeshire, Place Mill at Christchurch, and Woodbridge (Suffolk) are other examples. Just as wind turbines have developed as our modern windmills, the Rance barrage across the river Rance in Brittany has been generating electricity in a carbon-free, sustainable way since 1966, although there have been some environmental concerns.

Wheatley

Start and finish point SP597058

We first ascend the slope of the Corallian Ridge on which Wheatley village is situated down to the Cuddesdon watermill, then climb again via the villages of Cuddesdon, Denton, Garsington and Horspath to the Wheatley windmill. There are good views of the Chiltern Hills scarp slopes and Wittenham Clumps.

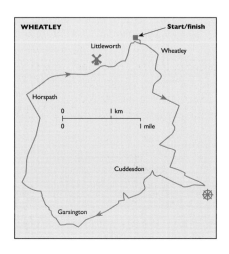

Distance: 9.0 miles (14.5 km).

Maps: Explorer 180 – Oxford, Witney & Woodstock.
Landranger 164 – Oxford.

Transport: Buses
- Wheatley, Oxford Stagecoach Company U1 (Brookes University).
- Heyfordian 103, 104, 275, 280 (goes to the Oxford Railway Station).
- 103/104 circular route from Oxford City to Cuddesdon, Denton, Wheatley and Horspath.
- Garsington T1. www.thames-travel.co.uk

Taxis: Wheatley
- Courtesy Cars. Tel: 01865 343575.
- Wheatley Taxis. Tel: 01865 876165.

Horspath
- PDQ Cars. Tel: 07850 329624.

Oxford
- ABC Radio Taxis. Tel: 01865 242424/770077.

Car Parking: Church Road Car Park (max. 4 hours) near the Wheatley, St Mary the Virgin Church bus stop. SP597058 (OX33 1LZ).
Overflow parking is available in The Merry Bells car park at SP598058 or along Church Road. (NB although The Merry Bells car park sign states that it is private, free but 4 hour limited car parking is allowed).

Accommodation/Public Houses/Refreshments:

Cuddesdon	• The Bat and Ball PH (serves morning coffee), B&B. Tel: 01865 874379. www.batball.co.uk
Denton	• Willow Cottage, B&B. Tel: 01865 874728. www.willowcottage.info
Garsington	• The Three Horseshoes, The Green. Tel: 01865 368666. www.thethreehorseshoesgarsington.co.uk
Wheatley	• The Sun PH, Church Road. Tel: 08712 238000.
	• The Railway Hotel, Station Road. Tel: 01865 872889. www.therailwaywheatley.com
	• The King & Queen PH, High Street. Tel: 01865 873443.
	• Crumbs Café, High St, (closed Sundays). Tel: 01865 874170.

Wheatley High Street
We pass Mott House and No. 88, the imposing Greystones, on the right. Roald Dahl's daughter Tessa, used to live at The Old Forge House, No. 99, on the left. We admired the steep stone doorsteps. On the right, Cromwell House is so named as Oliver Cromwell's daughter was married at Holton Manor, near Wheatley and it is said that a cupboard was taken from the Manor and installed here. Cromwell neither stayed nor lived here! The building stone is a deep yellow colour and called Wheatley stone, a medium grained, hard, Corallian limestone.

Leave the car park on the uphill side to turn right (E) past St Mary the Virgin Church. Turn right again, down through The Merry Bells car park and follow the sign downhill to the library. At the road, turn left (E) along the High Street.

On reaching Friday Lane turn right across the space that is Crown Square, named after the Crown Inn. The hunt always met in this square. Friday Lane gets its name from a Mr Friday who used to have a shop at the bottom of the lane. Go up Mulberry Drive, then turn left at the junction onto Beech Road and follow it to its end. At the start of Elm Close, turn right up Jackie's Lane which climbs between hedges. There is evidence of medieval ridge and furrow ploughing in the fields to the right and left. By looking back, above the spire of St Mary the Virgin Church, Beckley radio mast can be seen. The tall, square tower block to the left (N) is the Wheatley Park site of Brookes University, and beyond that is Arncott Hill south of Bicester. At Castle Hill Farm go through the gap beside the metal gate and through the farmyard. The white cattle are Limousin, originating from central France. Turn left (SE) on a track to cross the brow of Castle Hill, then after 600 yards, on beginning to descend, turn right (SW) at a crossroads of paths, even though the track (not a public right of way) continues ahead.

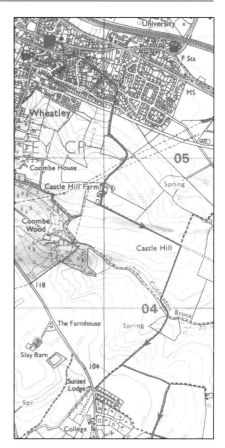

Castle Hill

The name Castle Hill is a corruption of Grasswell, which was so-named as the overgrown bath-house ruins of the wealthy Romano-British farmers occupying the villa estate suggested a grassy well. Castle Hill Farm is still Wheatley's main working farm. In September we saw, among the crops, red poppies and white bladder campion, with skylarks singing overhead.

The soil at the top of Castle Hill is sandy due to the limestone base. Where the soil changes to clay at lower levels, springs emerge as the water meets the impermeable clay. Springs are marked on the lower slopes north, south and east of Castle Hill. From the top of the hill the long ridge of the Chiltern Hills scarp slope can be seen with the BT Stokenchurch Tower visible to the south east.

Descend to Cuddesdon Brook (a tributary to the River Thame), turn left, then after 150 yards, turn right before the track veers to the left, over a footbridge (SW) hidden in the hedge. Go up the hill (SW) over a stile, then beside a planted hedgerow. We spotted spindleberry with its pink fruit, rosehips, dogwood, old hawthorn and guelder rose. Half-way up the slope, turn left, at SP601036, along the contours of the hill (SE, 110°), then at the T-junction of footpaths, turn right (S) not down the hill but climbing gently uphill for 350 yards. On approaching a clump of trees on the right of the path turn left at a crossroads of paths (SE, 110°) to descend towards the valley bottom. At the first field boundary hedge, the OS map shows a small dogleg right and left, but the farmer has marked the track directly south east, so continue in that direction bearing slightly more to the right and aim for the right hand side (S) of a small wood.

We noticed that there were many tiny slots of muntjac deer also using the footpath!

Leave the field by climbing a stile onto the road, turn left and walk for 75 yards down towards Cuddesdon watermill.

Muntjac deer slots

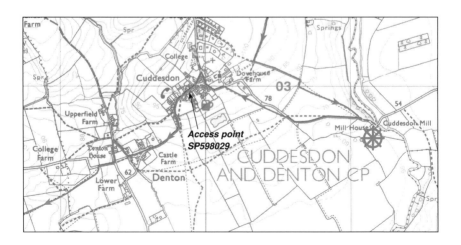

Cuddesdon Watermill

There has been a mill on this site since Anglo-Saxon times. The present, tall 18th-century stone building on the River Thame was originally for grinding corn. There is a date stone of 1716 on the right side of the bottom middle window. The Mill House is to the right and there are extensive water meadows either side beside the mill leat. A leat is a man-made channel diverted upstream from the main course of the river and therefore higher to provide the force of water for the mill wheel (*see illustration, p.12*).

Fifty yards further along the road, there is a twin-arched bridge made of dark industrial bricks over the River Thame. The land around the mill is private so take care when walking on the narrow road.

Retrace your steps up the slope (W) along the small road passing the stile we used earlier. Follow the road (W). (NB we could not find the short footpath shown on the OS map to the north of the road.) Just after the right-hand bend in the road, and 10 yards beyond the village sign, turn left at a footpath signed 'Cuddesdon ½' and go over a footbridge. Take the right of the two paths and follow it (NW) keeping to the right side of the field near the road, aiming for the church in **Cuddesdon**.

History of Cuddesdon
The origin of the name is from Cutha, a Saxon king. A large burial mound of about 600 AD, excavated in 1847, was of an exceptionally important man. This is indicated by several skeletons of corpses set out radially around the barrow who were laid face-down with their legs crossed and their heads pointing outwards, in a similar fashion to finds at Sutton Hoo, Suffolk. The people would have been the victims of sacrifice during the funeral. Inside the barrow were two swords, a garnet-studded fragment of bronze, and two Kentish blue glass bowls. One of these pieces of luxury Anglo-Saxon glassware was spotted in 1971, full of primroses, on a mantelpiece in Northamptonshire! It is now in the Ashmolean Museum. (Blair, J. *Anglo-Saxon Oxfordshire* (1994)). The barrow was in the grounds of Cuddesdon Palace, the former seat of the Bishops of Oxford. Ripon College, an internationally famous Anglican theological college, now occupies the site. Recently, a prize-winning, modern, oval-shaped chapel was built, well worth the 200 yard diversion (S) along the road from SP599031.

For visiting information (weekdays), Tel: 01865 874404. enquiries@rrc.ac.uk

At the road turn left alongside a high wall to arrive at a small green. A visit to Cuddesdson Church is worthwhile. The Norman doorway has chevron carving on it. On leaving the churchyard walk uphill past Church Cottages to the High Street to turn left (or right if visiting Ripon College) to go through the village.

Access point: Cuddesdon village 3.7 miles. Pub, B&B, bus. SP598029.

Pass The Bat and Ball Inn, the Old School House and then, just past the Village Hall on the left, is a recreation ground where we enjoyed a thermos of coffee. Continue SW past Vine Cottages on the right with their hooped metal railings and down the hill, ignoring the footpath leading to the right, to **Denton**. This route, via the road, gives us the opportunity to see the village green of Denton.

At the green, with Manor House Farm on the right, bear right (SW) across the green to go under the horse chestnut tree to a small clapper bridge over the brook. A clapper bridge is the dialect term for 'a rough or natural bridge across a stream', in this case it is a large piece of limestone. Do not take the stile ahead, but turn right alongside the brook (where there are carpets of snowdrops in spring) then sharp left (S) at the road.

On the right are the high walls of the originally 16th-century Denton House and to the left are the 17th-century stables, with a handsome cupola and weather vane. A friend of the author was evacuated here as a young child during World War II. We admired the lead drainpipes with their fish spouts on the wall of Denton House. There is a Baroque doorway with its characteristic broken arch.

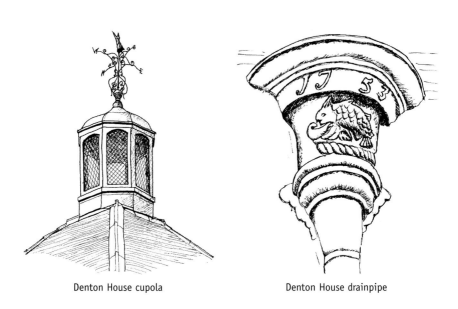

Denton House cupola   Denton House drainpipe

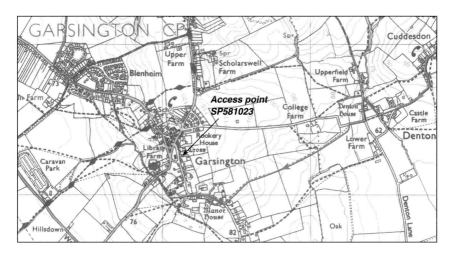

Continue beside the wall to turn right (W) on the road to Garsington. After 110 yards, turn left over two stiles on a footpath SW. Continue keeping in the middle of the field, parallel to the right-hand fence, climb the hill and pass through the hedge. Go through the next field boundary and continue climbing the hill towards the houses of **Garsington**.

Arable Field Margins
A notice explains that the wide rough-grass perimeters of the field provide a traditional habitat for ground-nesting birds, small mammals and invertebrates. Flowering plants provide a nectar source for the butterflies and other insects. Please avoid treading on these areas to protect the wildlife.
In the third field, just before the village, in September we walked through the most amazing array of wild flowers. The field had been planted with red clover, chicory, rest-harrow (so-called because its tough root could stop or arrest a harrow), birdsfoot trefoil, commonly known as 'bacon and eggs', yarrow and violet-coloured lucerne.

Rest-harrow

Climb a stile beside a metal gate onto the road and turn right. We admired the big old ash tree in Greystone House garden. On following this road (Southend), the outbuildings of Garsington Manor are approached.

Beside the road is a large barn, and on the right is a small granary of brick and timber supported on staddle stones, which stopped rats climbing into the grain (see Brill walk, p.29). This granary has been converted to accommodation but has no plumbing.

On the left, through the pillared gateway, is Garsington Manor, the former venue of the outdoor Garsington Opera, now moved to the Wormsley Estate in the Chilterns. On the right is a house, 'Home Close', with its yew hedges.

Garsington Manor

Garsington Manor was built in Tudor times on land owned by Thomas Chaucer, son of Geoffrey Chaucer, and was at one time called 'Chaucers'. Later it was owned by Lady Ottoline Morrell of the Bloomsbury Group, who entertained writers and artists such as D.H. Lawrence, Aldous Huxley, Seigfreid Sassoon, T.S. Eliot, Virginia Woolf, and Bertrand Russell who became her lover. A memorial to her by Eric Gill is in St Mary's, the parish church, on the left side of the south door. The gardens are in Italianate style and are occasionally open to the public.

Contact the head gardener, Tel: 01865 361234.

Follow the path beside the road past the Manor. Do not enter the high raised path on the right side of the road, but take the path bearing left downhill from the main road, beside the ancient fish ponds, through a wooden kissing gate, then bear right to cross a meadow to St Mary's Church where there is a good view of Wittenham Clumps. From the church, go (NW) down stone steps keeping on the right side of the field to a kissing gate. Follow the enclosed path to cross a road called Pettiwell (referring to a spring). Continue on the footpath to pass left of Knoll House over a Cotswold slab stile. Again follow the footpath along the edge of the field with views of Oxford city and Cowley (W).

Garsington

The name Garsington comes from the Anglo-Saxon *Gaerse-don* 'grassy hill'. Much of the village's history is recorded on the noticeboard on the green near the pub. For example, market gardening became a speciality in the 19th century and was taught as a subject at school. One of our walking group told us that her neighbour can remember his father taking vegetables on a horse and cart to the Oxford market in the 1920s. The present primary school was built on the site of one of the 15 former market gardens. Water was plentiful, since the site of Garsington arose due to the numerous local springs, reflected in such names as Pettiwell and Scholarswell Farm.

Go through the field boundary over a stile to keep due north in the middle of the field. (On the right is an old orchard with an enormous holly tree). A white-painted, steep-roofed cottage is a good landmark. We noticed how fine the soil is here. Go over another stile, along an enclosed path and down a driveway to the road.

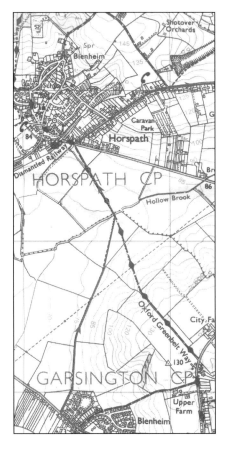

Access point: Garsington, The Green, 5.4 miles, bus, (300 yards from route). SP581023.

Turn left along the road and after 50 yards go through a metal barrier on the left to follow the path behind a hedgerow. Where the hedgerow ends follow the footpath, then the road verge for 0.3 miles, to turn right onto a footpath marked 'Horspath 1' (NE) on the same route as 'The Roman Way', a long-distance footpath going north to Alchester, the Roman military fort near Bicester.

This is an old green lane and we spotted ash, hawthorn, elderberry and sloe in the big hedges. When we arrived at an unharvested field of beans it was thick with house martins that were feeding on insects in September.

Continue along beside the hedgerow through two fields then, at a wide gap to the right (SP575038), bear left (NE), cross the field in which there is a telegraph pole. Go towards the hedge and willow trees of Hollow Brook (NW, 332°) aiming for the village of **Horspath** in the distance. Cross the bridge, to go up the left side of a field, through a gate and between horse paddocks onto the road. Cross the road with care and start to climb up Gidley Way opposite.

A bat hibernaculum

At Butts Road, it is possible to make a 1 mile diversion to visit a wildlife conservation area. Butts refers to the medieval times when the men built a large heap of soil and used it as a target (*see Brill walk, p,29*). The men practised for both the longbow and the crossbow. It was a legal requirement to practise on a Sunday and it was only in 1960 that the law was repealed. Before the railway bridge turn right via a kissing gate into the Wildlife Conservation Area. There is a circular route through the woodland. We noticed the red, gingery colour of the soil and there were arum lilies and the male fern whose leaves look like a badminton shuttlecock. We saw the bat hibernaculum, in this case in a blocked-up tunnel, where four species of bats hibernate. We returned beside the wetland area with glaucous sedge growing in the dampness. Leave the wildlife area, turn left and retrace your steps back to Gidley Way.

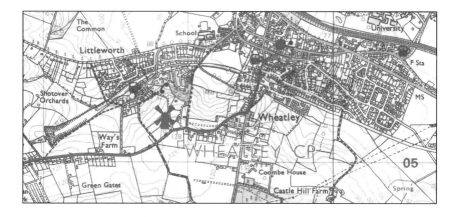

Turn left (NE) to continue along Gidley Way, and near the edge of the village pass Sandy Lane on the left where there is the first glimpse of Wheatley windmill to the east. Cross to the right-hand grass verges of the ribbon development and on to where the road turns sharp left. Enter Windmill Lane, an unmade-up track with bracken growing beside it. Continue on to the Wheatley windmill. Please respect the privacy of the owners of Mill House and their drive.

Wheatley Windmill

There were originally two windmills on this site: a post mill, which was on the opposite side of the lane, and the existing tower mill. The octagonal shape of this 18th-century tower mill is unusual. There are only two or three such towers in the UK. It ground wheat, but also yellow ochre from the pits on nearby Shotover. This yellow ochre was used as the pigment for medieval paintings and the characteristic yellow of the old Oxfordshire farm wagons in the 19th century.

Stone floor

The mill has been fully restored and won an award in 2010.

Open certain Sundays 2–6, May–October, tea and cakes served. Please check: www.wheatleymill.co.uk

Descend Windmill Lane with the view of the square tower block of Brookes University ahead towards the village of **Wheatley**, to turn left at the junction Ladder Hill — a field name meaning 'steep land' (it was excellent for sledging in the snow of December 2010!). Pass The Railway Hotel, so called as the Cowley to Thame railway, opened in 1864 but closed in the Beeching cuts of 1963, crossed here. Kelham Hall Drive was built over the site of the station. The pub houses railway memorabilia. Continue descending Ladder Hill to take the narrow Bell Lane on the right, down to the High Street. To the right are the shops and Crumbs Café. Turn left along the High Street and just before The King & Queen pub, turn right to climb uphill into the Church Road car park.

The Round House

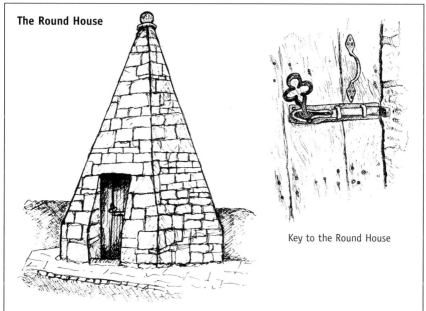

Key to the Round House

On the uphill side of the car park on Church Road 150 yards to the left, it is possible to see a small stone building just beyond the crossroads. This is the village lock-up or keep, which was a temporary holding place for those arrested before they were taken to the Justices. It was built in 1834 and is a six-faced pyramidal round house. In its day it was as much a symbol of class division, social unrest and economic recession as it was of a village with a drink and petty crime problem. (*The Story of Wheatley and Holton Park*, 2000.)

The Future

At their peak there were about 500,000 watermills and 200,000 wind-powered mills in Europe. However, these mills were limited by an unpredictable power supply, due to rivers freezing in winter, low river flow in dry periods and fluctuating wind speeds, and were eventually replaced by steam mills.

The beginning of the Industrial Revolution in the 19th century released human dependence on water and wind power. The Wessex Mill in Wantage (*see p.167*) is an example of a former water mill being replaced by a roller mill, now driven by electricity. Likewise the Combe Mill (*see p.68*) has evolved from water power to steam power to drive the beam engine and now uses electricity to power the saw mill.

Now with the current need to reduce our dependence on fossil fuels, hydro-electric schemes are being created (*see East Hanney Mill, p.71 and Mapledurham Mill, p.111*). The Minster Mill Hotel beside the River Windrush is the first hotel in the UK to produce electricity from its Archimedes screw installed in 2014. This produces sufficient electricity to supply forty-four of their rooms. The latest Oxfordshire project is the community-owned Osney Lock by the River Thames with a similar venture in Abingdon planned for 2016.

Just as water power has moved with the times, wind turbines are the next step in the development of the windmill. In 2014, power generated from wind farms and stand-alone turbines rose to meet 9.3% of the UK electricity demand.

Wind turbines

Wilton

Start and finish point SU280644

In Wiltshire, our route follows the Kennet and Avon canal to the Crofton pumping station. From there we continue to the site of Wolfhall, the ancestral home of the Seymour family made famous in Hilary Mantel's novel. We cross the open countryside to go through the village of Wilton and on up to Wilton windmill. The route goes through woodland and part of an original deer park to descend to the church and village of Great Bedwyn.

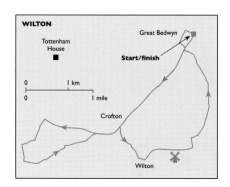

Distance: 9.3 miles (15 km).

Maps: Explorer 157 – Marlborough & Savernake Forest.
Landranger 174 – Newbury, Wantage & surrounding area.

Transport: Buses • Wiltshire Buses 20/21/X22. Great Bedwyn/Wilton/ Marlborough/Hungerford.
Rail • Bedwyn Station, First Great Western.

Taxis: Great Bedwyn • Bedwyn Cars. Tel: 07966 463809.
Marlborough • Arrow Taxis. Tel: 01672 515567.
Hungerford • First Direct. Tel: 01488 681182.

Car Parking: Great Bedwyn Wharf (SE of the canal). SU280644 (SN8 3PB).

Accommodation/Public Houses/Refreshments:
Crofton • Crofton Pumping Station, café. Tel: 01672 870300.
Burbage • Suddene Park Farm, B&B, caravan and camping. Tel: 01672 810296. www.suddeneparkfarm.co.uk
Wilton • The Swan. Tel: 01672 870274. www.theswanwilton.co.uk

Great Bedwyn   • The Cross Keys PH and B&B. Tel: 01672 870678.
www.thecrosskeyswiltshire.co.uk
• The Three Tuns PH. Tel: 01672 870280.
www.threetunsbedwyn.co.uk

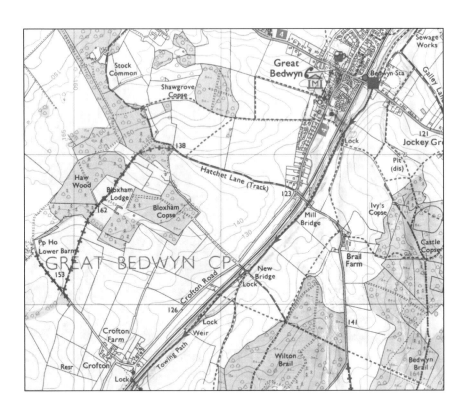

From the canal wharf car park exit left onto the towpath (SW) beside the Kennet and Avon Canal.

Continue following the path (SW) beside the canal to go beside Mill Bridge, where there used to be a watermill, and on under New Bridge where there are double tank traps. Pass the lock and bridge 100 and keep along the towpath towards the Crofton Beam engine with its tall chimney. It is well worth a diversion to visit the pumping station (*see p.192*) even if it is not in steam, either now or on the return loop from Wolfhall. On the left (S) is the entry of Wilton Water, part of the water supply for the pumping engine.

Kennet and Avon Canal
There are extensive reedbeds beside the canal where we saw a little egret fishing. The flora is varied; in March the pink butterbur was already in flower, in July the huge leaves of the rhubarb-like *Gunnera manicata* spread over the banks beside the blue water forget-me-not flowers. There are large concrete cylinders on the bridges over the canal. These are several groups of tank traps that were part of General Ironside's WWII strategy. He believed that the Germans would invade via the rivers and canals.

Bridge 99, tank traps

Monkey flowers

On the banks of Wilton Water we saw, in July, the distinctive heads of the yellow monkey flowers that favour damp conditions.

Access Point: Crofton Pumping Station 2 miles. Café. SU261623.

Crofton Pumping Station

To reach the pumping station go over the lock gates and into the tunnel built for the railway and up the steep flight of stairs.

This is the oldest working steam engine in the world, still performing the job it was built for. The beam engines were built 200 years ago to pump water to the highest point of the Kennet and Avon Canal, where it runs through Savernake Forest. The station originally relied on a well for its supply of water, but this could not be maintained, so with permission from Lord Ailesbury, who owned much of the land, the stream flowing from Wilton was blocked to form the large reservoir on the far side of the canal (Wilton Water). Lord Ailesbury, in compensation, requested a pipeline to supply his newly-built Tottenham House two miles away.

There are steaming days every month and on Bank Holidays during the summer, when visitors can see the huge tubular boilers being stoked and the pistons of the beam engines in action. The café is in the original enginemen's rest room.

Open March–October, 10–4.30. Tel: 01672 870300.

www.croftonbeamengines.org

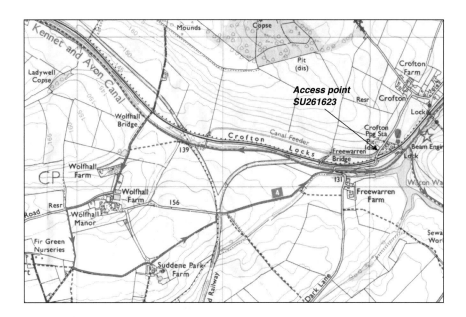

To resume the route, retrace your steps to the towpath (S) of the canal, and continue (W) past Freewarren Bridge and the Adopter's Lock to the site of a high dismantled railway bridge. Here, on the right side (N) of the canal, is the entry of the canal feeder of the pumped water that supplies the locks downstream. Follow the towpath to Wolfhall Bridge (103) to turn left (SW) onto a footpath and track climbing the slope. On the right side, before the wood there is a handsome square brick building with tall chimneys (Wolfhall Farm) that is thought to have been the original laundry of Wolfhall Manor. It was common practice to have the laundry separate from the main hall, partly due to fire risk.

Wolfhall Farm

Wolfhall Manor

Wolfhall Manor was the ancestral home of the Seymour family, Wardens of Savernake Forest, and of Jane Seymour, third wife of King Henry VIII. The king visited the old house several times, and it is probable that he hosted a celebratory wedding feast in 1536 in an ancient barn (which burned down in the 1920s). Prior to this, the barn still had the hooks on which the decorations and tapestries would have hung. The location of the barn was on the right side of the road opposite the farmyard (SU242618). A stained glass window commemorating King Henry and Queen Jane was moved from the mainly Victorian Wolfhall Manor to Great Bedwyn church. The name Wolfhall comes from the Saxon owner Ulph, and was the inspiration for the title of the prize-winning novel *Wolf Hall* by Hilary Mantel (2009). Broughton Castle near Banbury and Chastleton House near Chipping Norton were used in the televising of the novel. The farm buildings are now privately owned, so please respect the owners' privacy.

Continue to climb the track, through the farm gates where there is our first glimpse of Wilton windmill along the drive to the left (E). Go past the farm buildings in front of the ageing Victorian replacement of Wolfhall Manor and the former site of King Henry's barn.

Retrace your steps (N) to turn left onto a lane (W) to Burbage. There is an excellent view of Wolfhall Farm in the dip below. After 300 yards, turn left onto a footpath following the right side of a hedge. At a crossroad of paths turn left (E) at a bridleway sign along the top of a slope and continue past Suddene Park Farm and along the bridleway in the same direction (NE). There are views of the windmill on the brow of the hill. Descend the slope to the field end, then curve left, on the left side of an old hedgerow, to meet the lane by the remains of a dismantled railway. At the lane turn right to continue downhill, with a view of the Crofton Beam Engine ahead, to return to Freewarren Bridge. Go through the white gate on the right to follow the towpath to arrive opposite the pumping station.

Access Point: Crofton Pumping Station 5.5 miles. Café. SU261623.

Turn right over the exit of Wilton Water and onto a footpath (SE) beside it.

There are good chances to see birdlife here. We spotted a little grebe and the yellow-bellied grey wagtails in March.

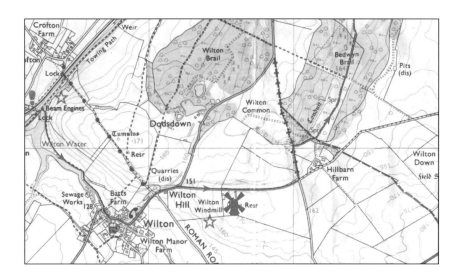

The path follows close to the water to meet the road into **Wilton** village opposite the pond. This is a clear, chalk, spring-fed pond and the water can be seen bubbling up in several places. Turn left through the village with its several thatched roofs and The Swan Inn on the right.

Wilton village pond

From the pub, bear left on the main road passing Wilton Manor Farm on the right side with its ancient barns and dovecote. Climb the hill, ignoring a road going right towards Marten. This road and the bridleway to the left form part of a Roman road from Winchester (Venta Belgarum) to Mildenhall (Cunetio), east of Marlborough, and on to Cirencester (Corinium). Continue up the road branching right, signposted Wilton Windmill and Shalbourne. After 400 yards, the windmill is signposted along a small track to the right on the summit of the hill.

Wilton Windmill (SU275616)
The mill stands high above the village of Wilton and is said to be the only working windmill in Wiltshire. With the building of the Kennet and Avon canal, the local watermills on the River Kennet lost their source of water. They were replaced by windmills, which in due course gave way to steam rollermills. The mill is a traditional five-floored tower mill with a fantail which turns the cap, ensuring that the sails always point into the wind. It has four sails in total; two patent which can be quickly activated and two common canvas sails, which have to be set before the mill starts to turn. The mill now produces stoneground wholemeal flour for sale at the mill or local retail outlets.

Source: www.wiltonwindmill.co.uk

Opening hours: Easter–September, Sundays and BHs 2–5 or parties by appointment. Site open all year.
Email: enquiry@wiltonwindmill.co.uk or Sue Challen, Tel: 01672 870202.

From the windmill turn right (E) along the high road with good views of the ridge of Inkpen Hill (E), then take a bridleway left opposite the entry of a road from Hungerford on the right. Follow the bridleway to take the first track right (NE) to bear right onto a footpath marked 'Great Bedwyn', then turn sharp left (NE) into Bedwyn Brail (brail is a term for an enclosed deer park within a forest) onto a gravelled footpath through the woods.

Where a footpath labelled 'Wilton Brail' leaves to the left, there is a wide, straight avenue across the valley. This viewpoint is across to Tottenham House, the former ancestral home of the Earls of Ailesbury, and beyond it, deep in the Savernake Forest, we could see, four miles away, the top of a tall stone column (the Ailesbury Column, SU231662).

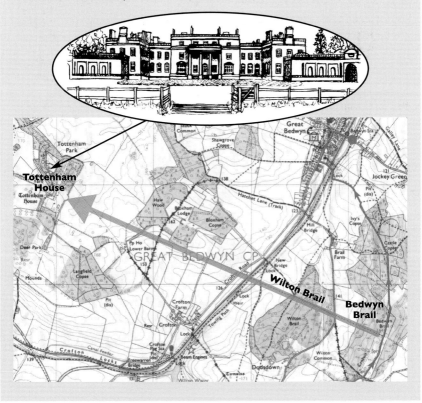

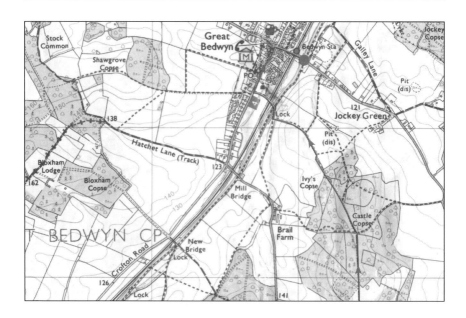

St Mary's Church, Great Bedwyn

The church is Saxon in origin, but has been restored. One of the stone capitals, however, still retains the charming carving of three heads, on the second column on the right of the nave, representing the stonemasons who built the church.

In the chancel is the fine Elizabethan tomb of Sir John Seymour, father of Jane Seymour, who lived at Wolfhall. At his feet is a carving of a lion, indicating his allegiance to the king. Above his tomb is the small carved window depicting the Imperial crown, the badge of Jane Seymour, and the Prince of Wales' feathers, which is the small window rescued from Wolfhall. In the choir vestry, in one of the low arched recesses, lies the stone effigy of a crusader knight, also with a lion couchant at his feet, and under the stone drain above him, a green man.

Window rescued from Wolfhall

In summer, teas are served in the vestry on Saturdays and Sundays, 3–5.

Continue in the same direction along the wide track (N) through Bedwyn Brail. Bear left (N). At the crossroad of tracks at Castle Copse follow the sign to 'Gt Bedwyn'. Pass through an open glade, then where the tracks divide bear left (NW, 320°) downhill along a narrow woodland path through Ivy's Copse and descend the slope on the right side of the hedgerow to reach the canal. Go over the canal bridge, then the river, cross the railway track with great care, and go towards the church tower at **Great Bedwyn**. We noticed watercress growing in the waters of the River Dun north of the canal. Take the footpath that leads into St Mary's churchyard.

On leaving the churchyard, take the path past a remarkably well-preserved preaching cross that still bears the vestiges of the original deep red, viridian green and white paint. Turn right into the village street past Pear Tree Cottage to arrive at a former stonemason's yard (now a shop and post office) on the left. Outside the shop is a slate showing a stonemason's costs.

```
REPAIRS TO A MONUMENT

CORRECTED THE TEN COMMANDMENTS          110
EMBELLISHED PONTIUS PILATE AND PUT NEW
RIBBON IN HIS BONNET.                    20
PUT NEW TAIL ON ROOSTER OF ST. PETER
AND MENDED HIS COMB                      25
REPLUMED AND REGILDED THE WAY OF
THE GUARDIAN ANGEL.                     155
WASHED THE SERVENT OF THE HIGH PRIEST.
AND PUT CARMINE ON HIS CHEEKS.           10
RENEWED HEAVEN. ADJUSTED THE STARS.
```

Stonemason's costs

Continue on to the crossroads at the small village green and turn right down the slope to pass the railway station on the left and on over the bridge to return to Bedwyn Wharf.

Maps
All maps reproduced from Ordnance Survey Mapping on behalf of
The Controller of Her Majesty's Stationery Office
© Crown Copyright.
Licence Number 100036702

Photographs
Front cover: Pitstone windmill
Back cover: (*top row, l–r*): Tysoe windmill; Ardington watermill;
Great Haseley windmill.
(*second row, l–r*): Ford End watermill (on the Pitstone walk);
Chinnor windmill; Stadhampton watermill (on the Great Haseley walk).